Investing

For

Your Life

Investing
For
Your Life

Provide yourself security
Through investing.

By

Chandler Deyo

ISBN 978-0-6151-6740-4

Dedication

This book is for, and dedicated to, those that work hard and want to be responsible in their lives.

Table of Contents

Dedication   v

Forward   x

Goals of the book   xi

Chapter 1   What is investing.   1

Chapter 2   Dividend and interest is   11
             the name of the game.

Chapter 3   Money, money, money   15
             over time.

Chapter 4   Technical sections.   25

             Section 4.1 Not so Boring Bonds   26
             Section 4.2 Closed-end income funds   34
             Section 4.3 Certificates of deposits   36
             Section 4.4 EE savings Bonds   38
             Section 4.5 Treasury securities   41
             Section 4.6 Preferred stocks   43
             Section 4.7 Dividend paying stocks   44
             Section 4.8 Real-estate Investment   47
                         Trusts (REIT's)
             Section 4.9 Master limited   50
                         Partnerships (MLP's)
             Section 4.10 Royalty trusts   52
             Section 4.11 Business development   53
                          companies (BDC's)
             Section 4.12 Stock options   55

Chapter 5   Liquidation preference   58

Chapter 6   Blueprint for investing   65

Chapter 7   Meet your broker on-line   71

Chapter 8   Advanced research   74

Chapter 9   Example portfolio's   83

Chapter 10   You and your websites   90

Chapter 11   401 type accounts   95

Chapter 12   Tickers, tickers, tickers   97

Chapter 13   The end of the beginning.   100

Tables & Graphs

Graph 1. Real Growth of Money   23

Table 1. Moody's Long-term Debt Ratings   29

Table 2. Moody's Short-term Debt Ratings   29

Table 3. Moody's Default Probabilities   31

Graph 2. Treasury Yield Curve   42

Investment Categories   66

$50,000 portfolio   85

$100,000 portfolio   88

Forward

This book is about taking financial responsibility for oneself. It's about learning, investing and dreaming about future goals and aspirations. It's meant for the small, new or young investor. Those that could be getting more out of their hard earned money. Money and wealth are the vehicles that get us to where we want to go in life. It's not about saving and spending money. It's about planning and achieving. Our lives would be empty if our primary goal was to make money. Although, when one doesn't have any money, it seems like money is the end all. The less money we have, the more we envy those who do have it, and lust after its sometimes crippling aspects.

This book is about planting the seed for future happiness. It's about teaching the aspects of investing and obtaining wealth, that will allow us to become responsible for oneself. Having income independently will allow greater flexibility in our lives and if the time comes unexpectedly, will provide some level of security, with the loss of a job.

It's crucial to develop these ideas and techniques at an early age. Unfortunately our education system is almost nonexistent on this topic. By becoming knowledgeable in investing at an early age, we become more confident and successful later in life. But don't give up hope if you're older, it's never too late to start investing.

Goals of the Book

Just like in business and in our personal live, it's important to set goals. Here are the goals of this book.

1. To develop a sense of being self-reliant.

2. To learn how to take financial responsibility for oneself.

3. To learn about the basic income investments that are available.

4. To create a confidence and to unravel the mysteries of investing.

5. To show a specific real life example on the growth of money over time.

5. To give specific direction on the type of tools and resources available for investing.

6. To give a specific sequence of investment types to begin investing.

7. To start investors on a path to achieve their dreams and aspirations.

Chapter 1

What is investing.

*M*y definition of investing is this; giving one's resources, mostly money, to individuals, governments, businesses, or other institutions for the purpose of enriching or improving those entities and getting back those resources with a profit, preferably periodically.

It's really not that complicated. With so many ways to invest and so many people making suggestions and so much information floating around, one would think that we should all be experts. But unfortunately the modis aprerendi seems to be, look for that great stock tip, take your $5000, plunk it down and hope for the best. This seems to be the connotation for investing. I realize it's appealing to dream about doubling or tripling your money in 30 days. I know the information came to you by a reliable source, but also what you know, is that this is not investing, this is playing the low odds, gambling. There are many people who would like you to do just that, but, I don't need to tell anyone, this is not investing.

The goal of the investor, as stated in the definition, is to give up resources, in the hope of getting a return for the risk. Therein lies the " art of investing". **For me and other investors, this is the fun of investing. Researching your investment, assessing the risk, and getting a periodic return.**

It takes time and energy to research the entity that will receive your resources. This can be a learning experience and is really the core of investing. This is what I mean when I say, "Be an active investor."

Once again, we hear all the talk, for example maybe in technology, maybe some specific memory device company. You probably feel skirted because you know nothing about memory devices, but once again, the information came from a reliable source so you bite.

Here's an alternate consideration, invest in something you know or like. We all have some interest. Let me use a couple of examples. The automobile industry is a big one. You may have a great interest in cars. You may know who's doing well, who has the best products. Take Toyota, GM, Ford etc. Go to their websites, go to investor relations, you know, start kicking the tires. Your goal here is to figure out how I get a piece of the pie. I'll want to get in on this action. How do I minimize my risk and get a good return. I will go into detail later on what to look for when accessing a company. Suffices to say, as an example, you choose Toyota. After making your investment, you should feel good about your piece of Toyota. As a Toyota vehicle goes by, you should see dollar signs. Pay attention to news reports on Toyota. Remember, what's good for Toyota, is now good for you. If Toyota does well, you also benefit. Toyota is no longer some big bad corporation; you are lending them your money, you want to see them succeed. You are part of the economy. You are no longer some helpless little person. Rejoice!

I will use another example. If you're the shopper and an investor, you probably know the best products if you do your homework when shopping. What products are good, what taste great. How about Land O' Lakes, Kraft Foods, etc. Here's another opportunity to get your piece of the pie. What new products are coming on the market? Are they good? As a consumer, would you buy their products again? This gives you some clues to future profitability. Also go to their website, go to investor relations. Read the quarterly statements. Listen to the company statements. I'll go into more detail later on what to look for in the financial statements. In this analysis you're doing, there is no magic. There is no right or wrong answers. No one has any advantage over you unless they have inside information, which is illegal. You want to go further, read the opinions of others. Also I will go into detail later on bond ratings which would be very helpful. So as a result of all your efforts, for example, let's say you invest in Land O' Lakes. Hey, let the butter flow. Pay attention to their policies; are they good to their employees? Watch your neighbor's grocery bags. You should see dollar signs when they buy Land O' Lakes butter. When Land O' Lakes does well, you benefit. You are part of the economy. You are getting your piece of the pie. Enjoy your Land O' Lakes interest checks when you receive them. Rejoice!

The point here is that investing is getting involved with the people, governments or companies that you have an interest. Investing is accessing the products or services and making an intelligent opinion as to the probability of making a profit on your resources. The tips I enjoy are those from my wife, children or friends. Tips not on which stock is hot but which product is hot. Why would you invest in something you

don't know or unwilling to learn. Our economy is filled with
all sorts of industries. Surely you can invest in something that
appeals to you or you have an interest in learning. The list is
endless but let me give you some other ideas of what I mean.
Jeans, clothes, tires, coffee, oil, propane, games, sports, golf,
hats, vacuum cleaners, steel, flowers, gardeners, shopping,
cigarettes, real estate, apartments, shopping centers, schools,
water treatment plants, colleges. As I said, the list is endless.
But what interests do you have, or better yet what do you want
to learn about. Go for it. Get your piece of the pie. Don't be a
victim. Take financial responsibility. Be a part of the
economy.

     A few years ago my mother-in-law kept telling us how
she enjoyed going to lunch at Friendly's. Other family
members expressed the same information. I decided to see if I
could get a piece of Friendly's. They are a restaurant that
features ice cream deserts. I searched and found they had some
corporate bonds on the secondary market. I researched the
company and found that they didn't have exactly stellar
financials, but realized they had a good product and would get
through their difficulties, so I purchased 10 bonds. I receive an
interest check every six months for $418.75. Quit regularly we
partake of their sundaes.

     I'd like to mention another small investment that my
wife and I have, this investment got me started in corporate
bonds. We bought two bonds of Mrs. Fields cookies. You
probably heard of them. They usually are in malls and
shopping centers. I didn't specifically go looking for them, but
saw the bonds for sale on the secondary market with a great
discount. Up to that point I don't think I had even bought a
cookie from them. We would walk past and would always see
people walking around with these big chocolate chip cookies.
I went to their website and saw that they were having some
difficulties and that is why the bonds were at a discount. Don't
worry at this point if you don't understand the jargon, I will go

into detail later in the section for bonds (section 4.1). We went to the mall and purchased a couple of the cookies, we realized that these are really good cookies. It was a little risky investment but at this point I was willing to take the risk, did my homework, and decided to buy two bonds at $750 each. That's a total investment of $1500. The coupon rate was 10% which gave me interest payments of $200. Since corporate bonds pay off every six months, I get a check of $100 every six months. We now occasionally buy a cookie at the mall and enjoy our investment returns. It was fun learning about the cookie industry and the good products that Mrs. Fields creates. This investment is not going to make me rich but it fits in my plan and I took a good opportunity. I'm not going to sweat about the investment. I will leave it and collect the interest payments until the bond matures and I get my resources returned in addition to the discount that I paid.

So this is the essence of investing; doing research, understanding the product or service, and making that leap of faith. Nobody can tell you if you're doing the right thing. There are signposts along the way that help guide you. As you probably can guess already, my methods for investing are to do your homework, take the leap and reap the rewards. I don't want to constantly go back and spend endless hours buying and selling, buying and selling. My method leaves little room for pure speculation and hopes of rapid increase in value. It may be classified as a diversified aggressive high yield fixed income investment plan. The reason I preferred this approach, is because I want to see some return on my investment, regularly. Buying a stock for merely the speculation of share price rise leaves few options. Either sell or buy more. If I have an investment that pays dividends or interests, I have many more options. I can spend the return, reinvest the return, buy more, or sell. I really believe that the days of stock speculation will be practiced by fewer and fewer individual investors.

Investing like anything else is a personal thing. Since most of us are working people, we don't have a lot of time to spend on investments. Therein lies the problem with active investing. How can I stay up on all of the information that is needed to adequately manage my resources? If you read books on the stock market that claim to have the right strategy you become numb to the jargon and technical detail required. This is one of the reasons that so many people just want that hot tip. Please tell me what stock to buy, but then, tell me when to sell, and then where to put the money after sale, it goes on and on. There are some newsletters that will tell you when to buy, what stock to buy and when to sell. There are methods for investing that says, sell if it reaches 5% below your cost, sell 8% below your cost, buy more if it falls 10% below your cost, keep buying more if it falls 20% below your cost. Of course there is the seasonal average, summer surges, super bowl predictions and Election Day outcome performance. All of these methods have been researched and have found some statistical significance. I have to come clean and report that I have, for many years read and studied many of them, and yes, tried many of them. Usually this great enthusiasm and hope dwindled to nothing more than a lost dream. Dreams of becoming rich, dreams of finding the golden ring, dreams of thinking that some way I would beat the system and find fame and fortune in the stock market.

I don't discourage this pursuit of information or desire to find that investment panacea. In fact, I encourage knowledge and information gathering. But if you are going to take $5,000 and put it down on a certain stock because a certain person wins the White House, then I have a problem. These technical approaches to investing have a place. They can be fun and of course could make you a profit if analyzed properly. My main concern with all of this advice and technical recommendations that are made, do not take into account the investors situation. It's one thing to spend $5,000 on a common stock, with no

dividend, and hope that the price will appreciate if you have
$500,000 in your investment portfolio. This may be the time to
take some risk, play that hunch. It's quite another thing
entirely if you only have $10,000 in your investment portfolio
and you're going to invest $5,000 in a common stock that
doesn't pay a dividend, and hope for some dramatic price
appreciation. This is what I mean when I say; take control of
your financial responsibilities. Learn enough so you can make
your own financial decisions. Hey, this is your life, your
security. The people making those suggestions may benefit
from your fall; at best they may have made an honest
assessment. But they don't know you, only you know you in
your investment life.

 This advice that we read in the newspaper and see on TV
is not a unique situation in the investment community. It's
pervasive throughout our culture, some of it is honest unbiased
information, and some of it is obviously self-indulgent and
potentially profitable to the provider. In his book, Who is
Looking Out For You, by Bill O'Reilly, there is great detail on
many, many instances in your life. He correctly points out that
many, if not most are clearly not looking out for you. So the
question remains, who is looking out for your financial future?
The answer is you. You have to take control of your resources.
I have no problem if you are in the camp that says all resources
are owned by society. There are many who believe that your
money and resources are the result of the hard work of those
before you. In fact, I agree to a point that, that this is the case.
We live in a fortunate time. Technology has made our life
easier. The computer and software have made investing
tremendously easier over the past 20 years. One can now do
research and acquire information at an amazing pace. I realize
that those before me have made it easier for me to invest and
subsequently have enriched my resources. I don't believe there
is any disputing that fact. I further have no problem if one
wants to leave all of their assets to society when they depart.

In fact, one of the richest individuals of our time, Bill Gates, said this about wealth "I am the steward of a share of society's resources, eventually; I'll return most of it as contributions to causes I believe in, such as education and population stability."

This is a very noble endeavor and I believe you have the same right to fund your favorite causes. Where I think most of us go wrong though, is that we are not good stewards of those resources while we have them. It's important to properly control the money we have. **We can obtain advice, we can learn from others' mistakes, but we must take responsibility for our financial future.**

There are two blatant examples in our society that illustrate this idea about giving advice and getting advice. The golf industry is notorious about giving advice to golfers without ever seeing their swing. TV, radio, magazines, manufacturers, etc. all are constantly giving advice on that great panacea. This will make you an expert golfer. This message is what you've been waiting for, this club will cure your slice, this ball will give you greater distance, and this swing thought will put you in the right mood. So as Bill O'Reilly might say, who's looking out for your golf swing? The golf ball manufactures, the pro golfer, or the golf course owner? Probably none of the above. The antithesis of this example is the medical community. It is set up such that certain kinds of medications cannot be prescribed unless someone investigates your condition, understands your health record, and looks at your history. In most cases, I believe your doctor is giving you unbiased information. People make mistakes but I think that most accept their doctor's judgment. But if you don't, you can go to someone else.

In summary, **it's important to understand that we live in a capitalistic society where we are allowed to participate in the fruits of our workers and producers**. Capital or money is needed for the investment of those producers. It's incumbent upon all of us to aid in that production by being

producers ourselves and investing in the hopes that profits
from those investments will further improve and aid our
financial future. The stability that you will achieve from
investing and taking control of your resources will allow you
flexibility and give you opportunities to pursue your dreams
and aspirations. It is an admirable goal to want to have
independent resources rather than relying on each paycheck to
support your endeavors.

I would like to end this chapter with commentary on a
biblical parable. The full text can be read in the bible in
Matthew 25:14-20 or another version is in Luke 19:11-27.

This old story has a few different versions, but the theme
remains the same. This parable has given me great inspiration
over the years. Even though it's just a story, I believe basically
it tells us we should strive to be good stewards of not only our
resources but also our talents. We should always be mindful of
our personal contributions and as the saying goes, "Be all you
can be."

The story goes something like this. A man, presumably
with enormous wealth, goes abroad but leaves some money
with his workers. In one version, he leaves five bags of gold
with one, two bags of gold with a second and one bag of gold
with a third. It's also stated that the resources are given to each
based on their capabilities. The man then leaves the country,
expecting his workers to manage the money wisely and
improve his positions. The first two, increase the value by
doubling what was given to them. The third decided that the
man was a ruthless businessman and would be upset if he lost
the one bag of gold that was given to him, so he buried it.
Upon returning from his trip, and learning the results of the
three, he awarded the first two but scolded the last for not
increasing the value of the one bag of gold. In fact, that poor
soul is now somewhere in the darkness waling and gnashing
his teeth.

When first reading this parable, it seems like there is no

compassion in the businessman. Besides, if we are to believe that the third has less capability than the other two, then why was he so upset when he received his one bag of gold? Maybe it's tough love, or maybe he was just a big bad conservative. I believe, the moral value of this parable is significant, it says no matter what capabilities you have, no matter how insignificant, or unimportant you are, it is morally, theologically, and fundamental, that we apply those talents in the best way you can. We must use what we have been given, such as the third person in the story. A talent is another word for money. In the parable, a talent is a unit of money. But I don't think the relationship between having talents, you know skills, is not that far remote from money. The story has a broad meaning, in that we should take advantage of our God-given strengths, but since the story uses money as its basis, I believe also that it is saying we should not squander our money, but should be good stewards. The parable ends with the message that we should increase our resources, but does not; discuss what is appropriate behavior for increasing those resources. I should think that all other moral and legal values should be followed. I don't believe it's saying that there is no limit to the behavior necessary to increase your resources.

11

Chapter 2

Dividend and interest is the name of the game.

*J*ust like in the song, Name of The Game, by the pop group Abba; in investing, the name of the game is dividend and interest. In an investing plan that highlights return, the primary goal is to invest in an entity and expect a return through periodic dividend or interest payments. If one invests and doesn't expect a return in the form of a dividend or interest payment, then the only way one can get a return is from an appreciation of the principle. In other words, when buying a stock with little or no dividend, it's incumbent upon some

future announcement, a big breakthrough, abnormally high
sales, great announcement about management, or a corporate
realignment. Some important or great thing has to happen in
order for the stock price to quickly appreciate in order for you
to get your quick return. That is called stock speculation. It
can be risky, and in addition, it takes time to research your buy
and sell and it has to be timed correctly. Of course you can get
a higher return if everything goes to plan. But then you have to
do it again, and again. What are the odds that every outcome
will come to fruition? Some people get a kick out of this type
of speculating. Some people are good at it. In my opinion, this
kind of investing should be for the high end investor, someone
who has years of experience in this type of game, and for those
who already have an established base of good investments and
wants to take, probably 5 to 10% of their funds, and have some
fun. This would be your don't matter money.

Something that must be understood about stock
appreciation is that in most cases it provides no real increase in
production output. This means that the real output growth is
not really increasing. This gain is not really bought and paid
for from real productivity improvements. If real sustained
productivity increases were being made, then the stock price
would not go back down. Keep in mind that you are on shaky
ground when a stock price appreciates very quickly. Of course
this is not always the case. So you have to ask yourself the
question before speculating, where is the appreciation that I'm
looking for, going to come from. If it is a fabricated increase,
then trod lightly.

**If on the other hand, if a stock has increased because
of an increase in dividend, then the increase is, so called
bought and paid for.** The only way this is not true, is if the
increase in dividend comes from capital instead of productivity
improvements. This however is an easy thing to spot (see
section 4.1 on bonds).

The other potential way to invest in stocks that do not

return a dividend is to buy and hold. The idea with this type of investment is to buy a good stock and hold it for the long haul, maybe over years. The hope is that the company you pick will grow at a faster rate than the average growth rate of the economy. This takes time up front, but little additional time once purchased. So the really, big hope, is that you will pick a company that has something that its competitors don't have. Unfortunately the sad fact about this strategy is that, it's extremely difficult to pick a great stock. The fact is, most people would be doing well if they just meant the average return. In fact, statistics show that only 40% percent of fund managers beat or meet the stock average returns. These are people who do this for a living. The moral here, it is most difficult to pick stocks that provide a growth return. The odds are really stacked against the average investor. Stocks go up and stocks go down. They always have and they always will.

It is very instructive to see where stock prices and stock appreciation really comes from. Studies have confirmed that over 40% of stock returns over the long term have come from dividends. That's right, ho-hum dividends. Unfortunately, there are fewer stocks today paying dividends than in the past. In the early 1980's, 90% of the top 3000 stocks (Russell 1000 index), by capitalization, paid dividends. In early 2000 it dropped to 55%. The trend has been to ignore dividend paying stocks, but the data is clear, in that higher yielding stocks have significantly outperformed lower-yield or no-yield stocks over the long haul. I have included in the bibliography some of those studies that you can review.

Another way to look at it is that, receiving your dividend is money in hand. You can spend it, reinvest in the same company, or reinvest in another investment. To get your return from a stock that doesn't have a dividend, you must time the sale, such that you have an appreciation when you plan to sell it.

Bonds by their very nature are considered a conservative

investment because generally you get paid on a regular basis in the form of interest payments. It's no secret that bonds are a more secure investment and if managed correctly can be an almost guaranteed source of income. Of course, bonds are considered boring investments because they're not as flashy and they don't generally return high percentages, although it is possible to get a reasonably high return with a little risk, which will be outlined in the section on bonds (Section 4.1).

In summary, to achieve the long-term goal of having personal responsibility through financial success in investing, it is essential that investments be made in those entities that provide a return through dividend or interest payments. Speculative investments are reserved for a small percentage of your portfolio. These periodic payments may be used to pay bills, or reinvested to increase your resources, which in turn increases your return, or used occasionally to have fun. The bottom line, these returns should give oneself satisfaction, independence and self-reliance. As your resources and return increases over the years so should your self-reliance and independence. Relying on your paycheck for your sustenance and enjoyment should diminish over the years.

Chapter 3

Money, money, money over time.

*T*his is the chapter of the book where I divulge some of my investing history. Feel free to pass on this chapter. I'm including it to show how the accumulation of money over a long period of time can occur. **I want you to also understand that you have a financial life, not in addition to your normal life but one that should be in concert with your normal life.** Also that investing is a long-term proposition; hopefully my example will encourage those that want to develop self-sufficiency and independence. It's clear that not everyone will achieve the same level of net worth or independence, but the point here, is to see, that over the long haul, money will multiply and provide that self-satisfaction. I also provide the 5 biggest impacts on my financial life.

My investment life began around the age of 10 or 11. I don't remember exactly how old I was, but I have an approximate age of 10. This coincides with my, you might say employment, as an altar boy. That's right I was raised a Catholic and served the priests as an altar boy. I took over the daily altar boy job from my friend. He didn't want to do it any longer so encouraged me to take over. I said I would, so a meeting was arranged with our priest, Father Howard. He agreed that I could have the job, as long as I understood the responsibility. I would have to serve Mass every morning before school, Monday through Saturday. For my contribution I would get $.50 per Mass that I quickly calculated to be $2.50 per week. Father gave us his blessing as I left his office, I couldn't be happier. I was serving the Lord and getting paid for it. Wow!

Needless to say, this was good steady income. Now combining the money I made from mowing lawns in the summer and picking blueberries, I was able to have money, to spend and to invest. In the 1960s, EE savings bonds were introduced to students in the public schools. We could go to the post office, and buy a $.10 or $.25 stamp. The stamps would be put into a book and as soon as $12.50 worth of stamps was accumulated, we would bring the book back to the post office and we would obtain a $25 federal government EE savings bond. I can't tell you how static I was when I was handed in $12.50 and received $25 back. I realized that I had to hold the bond for some years but still to me, it was free money. I got a big kick out of this process. A little work on my part, collecting stamps by saving my money and then getting free money in my mind. After getting the bond I was ready to start collecting for the next bond. Very early in my

Page 17

life I already saw the relationship to working for an income, taking that income and purchasing an investment, and then collecting a return on that investment. There was a clear link between being responsible in your job and getting an income and using that income to generate more income. These savings bonds began my quest and enhanced my thirst for investing. What a country, the more money I gave them, the more I got back. My saying that I coined in my teens were, the more money you save the more money you will have to spend, because of the return. In my eyes saving was a way to salvation, at least salvation in my life.

My family came from very menial means and didn't have a lot of money. My father was a truck driver making barely enough money to support his growing family. My mother would spend the money on food very frugally. We had enough but nothing extravagant. My father was a quiet man, when I was growing up, but he did encourage the saving of money. He didn't mention many issues, but he did tell us, that saving was very important. So this investing that I enjoyed was hugely reinforced from my family situation. This only encouraged me to continue and gave me a great sense that I was on the right path.

Of course the amount of money that I was saving, wasn't going to make me rich. In fact, I had no plan at the time about what I was going to do with the money. Now, looking back, I realized that I was developing good habits, and if continued could bring bigger returns later in life. Besides developing good saving habits it also gave me a good sense of self dependency. I also remember having 15 or $20 in my wallet. This was a tidy sum of money for a teenager in the 1960s. Another really important aspect of money that I learned was that money wasn't the end all. Since I had a steady income I could budget my savings and still have plenty of money to buy model airplanes, clothes, and anything else I wanted. I felt like a really big dude because I could buy things

Investing For Your Life

I wanted and still go back home with my saving bonds sitting in my drawer.

In 1970 the Northern Adirondack Central School district was created out of three small rural school districts. My existing school, before the merge, was close by, and the church was on the way to school. It was convenient for me to finish Mass in the morning and get to school on time. Now my whole world was changing because I would have to be bused to another school some 12 miles away, this meant that my steady income was coming to an end. Since it was only the high school that would have to be bused, the tradition continued, like before. I selected a younger friend who I thought could do the job for Father Howard, we had a meeting in his office and he instructed my friend that he had the job, as daily altar boy as long as he understood his responsibilities. He must be on time for Mass every morning. I wished him well, and my steady income was gone.

However this fate that just stared me in the face would give rise to the second major impact in my financial growth. During the next summer, I was looking for steady income. I had odd jobs mowing lawns, etc., but I knew that steady income was important to be able to save and still have money to have fun with. I had heard that a farmer in a nearby town was looking for a few guys to help with the chores and work around the barn. Dairy farms were quite prevalent around my town, so I decided to give it a try. I knew it would be hard work, and probably long hours, but I equated that to a lot of money. Since I didn't know the man directly, I was a little hesitant to approach him, but did anyway. I figured my source of the information was correct, so I thought it would be a done deal. I remember pulling up in the driveway and he just happened to be coming out of the barn. I was very polite and told him that I had heard he was looking for a hired hand, and I was interested in the job. Even though it was many, many years ago, over 30 years ago, I can still remember seeing his face as I asked him the question. He was very cold, looked me up and down, and after about 30 seconds said something to the effect of, "No!" To myself I said, "Uh?" Outwardly, I tried to recover and make some conversation, but he wasn't interested. I walked away with my head down and remember thinking very clearly at this time. Here was a man with no education, telling me that I wasn't needed. I realized he had tremendous power over me. I had to work for people like him. My financial future depended on others like him. I would be beholden to others like him. This feeling gave me a sense of worthlessness.

Looking back on the situation. I'm sure the man never thought twice about it. He probably just was expressing his need at the time, because he didn't need a hired hand. I received something totally different from the experience. I wanted to be self-reliant. I wanted to be beholding to no one. I would make my own way. I would provide what I needed. I wanted nothing from nobody. Of course this was nonsense. In some respects, because there is a tremendous independency with others. This scenario, however, made a tremendous impact on my financial future. At some point, I wanted to be financially self-sufficient. This drove my desire in a financial sense, and also carried over to other parts of my life. Here I go world, I'm 16 and I'm independent.

The next big catalyst that occurred a few years later was the introduction of the Individual Retirement Account (IRA). The IRA started in the tax code in 1974. It was called the Employee Income Security Act of 1974, modifying IR codes 219 and 408. I was a senior in high school. I remember reading several articles about this new individual retirement account. Since your money grew tax deferred, a large amount of net worth could be accumulated. I remember seeing tables in a newspaper trying to entice people to take advantage of this program to increase the savings rate among our population. It would show these yearly investments, how they would multiply and in 20, 30, 40 years have enormous amounts of money. The chart would usually go to over $1 million. This period of time in my financial growth now gave me the blueprint for total independence. In my mind, at least, if I continued to save, it was possible for me to become a millionaire. This made a huge impression on my memory banks; it now showed me the light and gave me a goal to shoot for. I realized that it would take many years to do so, but the way I looked at it, in 30 years I can be a millionaire with a little saving or I can spend all my money and have nothing when the 30 years approached. There didn't seem to be any comparison. **In my mind it was crystal clear; the way to total self dependency was through savings.** I never really developed any sense of worship for money. Money in itself meant nothing. The idea of doing the things I wanted to do, when I wanted to do them, was my motivation for saving. I never developed a miser like attitude. I enjoyed spending my money, but I got joy from saving and seeing it grow also.

So here are the three major events that impacted my financial future and life up to this point in a nutshell. I got steady income and learned about investing in US EE savings bonds, had a monumental moment that showed me I must be independent, and saw through the use of an IRA the opportunity to increase wealth over time.

As I mentioned earlier, those saving bonds never really provided me with any real future in self dependency. They were gone after about two or three semesters in college. They did provide some initial resources, but mainly they were instructive. Like a lot of people, it was tough getting through college, financially. I had no opportunity to save money at this time in my life. My net worth now went negative as I had school loans. After going to college for two years I joined the Navy and spent four years as an electronic technician. I saved about $6,000 during those four years, and upon exiting the Navy went back to school and completed a degree in an

electrical engineering from California State University at
Fresno. Once again, I had two more years of no savings, since
I was attending college, but this time on the G.I. Bill. I was
able to get through the last two years and still have about
$2000 left.

So I was 26, had about $2000 in savings, (still a negative
net worth), and I was ready to go about my business as an
electrical engineer and save and pave my way to self
dependency. My starting salary out of college was $24,500.
This was a lot of money to me. It was an above average salary
and I knew that I could easily meet my saving goals.

As I saved my money, I began to expand my horizons on
different type of investments. I read a lot and had a number of
great mentors as coworkers at General Electric, where I was
working in the Military Electronics Division in Syracuse, New
York. These mentors were very conservative, and had saved
their money, spending time learning the trade of investing. It
was a very instructive time in my early investing career. I
developed very close friendships at GE, and they showed me
the ropes. They were many years my senior. Most of them the
age of my father. My father was able to instill the idea of
investing, but these guys were showing me how to invest. We
had numerous conversations and they treated me with much
respect and dignity. I learned a lot from these folks, I can say
that this was the fourth biggest impact on my financial growth.
I learned about interest rates and monetary policy and the
Federal Reserve and mutual funds and bonds to name a few.
They would tease each other respectfully, "did you reach your
hundred K yet?' The $100,000 plateau was an achievement, but
it was just the beginning. It is very difficult to reach a hundred
K, but things would happen exponentially after that. No one
bragged of their money, no one would show anybody up, they
had tremendous mutual respect for each other, and they
enjoyed passing information back and forth

So now it's time to see money grow. I have included the

years and amount of resources achieved. This is not a
hypothetical, this is the real thing. I selected intervals for the
purpose of the chart, but my records have a lot more intervals. I
generally would review and record my portfolio about once a
month. I lost my records between December 31, 1981 and
February 15, 1989, so that's why there are no data points
between those dates. I have included what I feel is beneficial
data. You can see that it takes many years to get your
resources going, and the early stages are important, because
you want to establish a good foundation. I will speak later
about specific investments. **The more you can save in the
early years, the earlier it will be in later years that you will
meet your goals.**

The two end points of the graph are:

December 31, 1981 $2,132.97

September 25, 1994 $100,591.00

Graph 1. Real Growth of Money

Portfolio Value Over Time

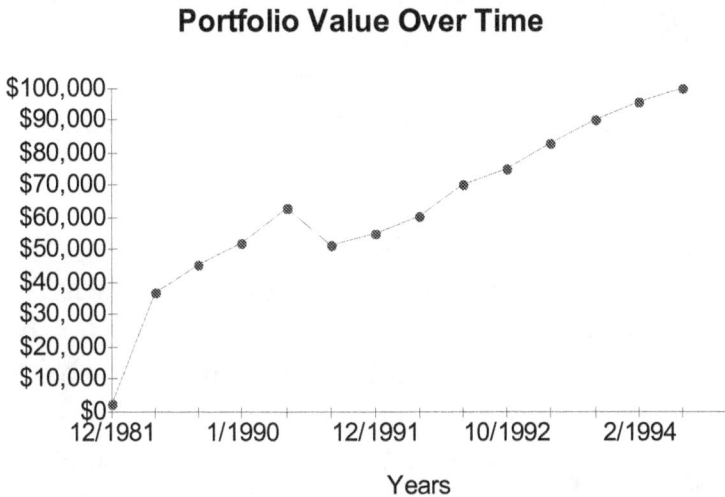

I hope you find this chart instructive. The moral here is that it takes many years for us, who start with nothing, to gain a lot of net worth. The thing to remember is that, your case may be different than mine. It's not important that you achieve your neighbor's numbers, what's important is that you provide to yourself self sufficient income. In all likelihood, most people will never have $1 million. Maybe $100 K or $200 K is realistic. Set your goals realistically. You can be a financial success at $10K. Remember, at 6% interest, 10K would bring 600 dollars a year in income. Depending on your salary, that could be an extra paycheck. $20 K could be two extra paychecks. **That's really the way you have to look at it. How much security are you able to bring to yourself.**

As you can see, I've concluded the chart at a $100 K. I believe this is far enough for anyone to get the point. It took 13 years to reach that plateau. Another reason I stopped the chart is because 1999 and 2000 the stock market went precipitately high and investments were mounting up quickly as this once-in-a-lifetime experience occurred. It doesn't serve any purpose here to explore the rise and fall of the stock market during those times in history. You may have a similar lifetime event in your financial life and you should pay attention to your investments for that purpose, but under ordinary circumstances, money will compound and the more you acquire the faster it grows.

This brings me to the fifth major impact on my financial career. During this time frame, the market in 1999 was growing very fast, well above any real growth rates for the economy. It also happened that the company I was working for, QUALCOMM also grew, in fact, faster than almost all other companies. For this reason, my stock portfolio and QUALCOMM grew at a very high rate. The next year it dropped at a very high rate. Somehow, I was able to manage the very choppy waters and come out in very good shape. This once in a life time period allowed me to increase my portfolio faster than I had anticipated. I can't say why fate put me here, at this time, to benefit from the situation. This occurrence will probably never happen again. However, looking back I feel the other major impacts were just as significant, in fact, they allowed me to handle the situation.

I hope everyone gets the same opportunities I have had, to mold their financial future. It's important to reflect and take advantage, of these signposts and friends that can guide you in your financial growth. I hope you have found my story instructive. Now get out there and make your own financial story.

Chapter 4

Technical sections

*T*he following sections are what I consider to be the technical section of the book. These sections give a basic understanding of many of the various forms of investments. It's meant not to be too technical, but should give you enough information to get you started investing in these various instruments. It is not considered to be totally comprehensive. As one invests in these various instruments, additional understanding and insight will be learned. Hopefully this information will entice you to obtain more information from other sources which will allow you to gradually increase your knowledge base.

Section 4.1

Not So Boring Bonds

Even though bonds may be considered boring and without the sizzle and excitement of stocks, they should be the bedrock of your investments. They have long been the conservative vehicle in investing, and they continue to be secure investments. If managed properly, one could put all their investments in bonds, because they are so flexible and diverse. Bonds may be issued by any organization in any industry in our capitalistic society. Besides the typical corporate bonds, bonds are issued by municipalities, all forms of governments, government agencies, banks and financial institutions. Since there are so many different types of bonds, it's easy to diversify in many industries and governments. The interest on most municipal bonds is usually tax free.

One of the disadvantages of bonds is that the prices of bonds generally move together. This means that if you only hold bonds, you could be diversified in many industries, but your total portfolio value could change dramatically as interest rates change. The reason for interest rates rise and fall may be quite complex, but one should not let this type of monetary policy cloud their investment choices. **The bottom line here is this; it's not important why interest rates go up and down, what you need to know as an investor is how the change affects your investments.** The good thing about interest rate changes is that they happen gradually and happen in one direction at a time. In a nutshell, the Federal Reserve which is the Bank of the United States sets the treasury interest rates. This is a lending rate that is sometimes referred to as the base rate. The present interest rate curve, called the Treasury

Yield Curve, can be seen in Graph 3, of section 4.5. These rates are set on a daily basis and are the basis for all other lending rates. So when the feds change the rates, it affects bond prices in the rest of our economy.

It's clear that the interest rate changes slowly over a period of time. Sometimes it takes years to make significant changes. That means you have plenty of time to assess your investments when interest rates start to change.

So now that we've established the fact that interest rates affect bond prices and that it happens over a long period of time, how specifically, does it affect prices? As interest rates rise, the prices of bonds go down. This would be the case for individual bonds. If one holds a collection of bonds, generally the total portfolio value would decrease. This would also be the case, if you own a bond fund or a mutual fund that owns bonds. Conversely, if interest rates go down, bond prices will go up. So the bottom line on interest rates may be summed up in this way. **Bonds or bond funds are going to decrease in value when interest rates rise and increase in value when interest rates fall**.

This now brings us to an important advantage in owning individual bonds over a bond fund. Even though the price of individual bonds may decrease when interest rates go up, the realized loss of capital from those bonds will only occur if the bonds are sold before maturity. If the bonds are held until maturity, then the bond holder will receive the par value. Since I believe bonds should be bought with the intention of holding until maturity, then the bond price has little importance to the investor. **In other words, if you buy individual bonds and intend to hold them until maturity, then you don't have to worry about interest rates.** However, if you own a bond fund, then you are forced to live with the new value of the fund until the interest rates begin to rise again, which could be longer than you plan to hold the fund.

What else affects the price of bonds? The biggest effect

on the price is the bond rating. Bonds are rated by an independent agency. In fact, there are multiple bond rating agencies. Two of the most popular are Standard and Poor's and Moody's. This very fact that each bond offering is rated is the reason that bonds are a great secure investment. Secure investment in the sense that, you obtain credible unbiased information on the bond before you purchase it. What this means to the investor is that the risk can be calculated. As you might expect, you will get a higher return for bonds that have a lower rating. In other words, the higher the rating the lower the return. This is logical because if you want to take a higher risk, you should get rewarded. Of course, your high risk choice could lead to a bond that goes in default (see Table 3). This means the issuer no longer pays the interest. There is an additional benefit in the bond rating system. There is a dividing line in ratings, where above the line is considered investment-grade and below the line is non investment-grade. What this means to the investor is that if you purchase a bond that is investment-grade, there's a very high probability that the interest payments (your return) will be made. As you get farther away from that dividing line, and you go lower in rating, the probability of default is greater. As you might expect a very low rating would equate to a very high return. Any bond that is rated below investment grade, below BBB(S&P rating), is referred to as junk bonds. However, not all junk bonds are equal. This is where an investor can do his homework and get a nice return. **Just because the bonds are rated junk doesn't mean the companies that issue those bonds are junk.** A lot of good companies and governments have their bonds listed as junk. It's worth researching to find a nice return, but you have to assure yourself that the risk you are willing to take is worth the return.

Table 1: Moody's Long-term Debt Ratings (maturities of one year or greater)

Investment Grade
Aaa – highest rating, representing minimum credit risk
Aa1, Aa2, Aa3 – high-grade
A1, A2, A3 – upper-medium grade
Baa1, Baa2, Baa3 – medium grade

Speculative Grade
Ba1, Ba2, Ba3 – speculative elements
B1, B2, B3 – subject to high credit risk
Caa1, Caa2, Caa3 – bonds of poor standing
Ca – highly speculative, or near default
C – lowest rating, bonds typically in default, little prospect for recovery of principal or interest.

Table 2: Moody's Short-Term Debt Ratings (maturities of less than one year)

Prime-1 (highest quality)
Prime-2
Prime-3
Not Prime

The other important thing to know about bond ratings is that they can change at any time. The rating agencies continue to monitor the financial health of the issuing agencies and companies. If something happens with the issuing agency, positive or negative, the rating can be moved up or down. As you can see, there are many ratings; therefore, it takes a long time, usually years for a rating on a particular bond to change dramatically. This is one thing you can do to monitor your investments. They both have free websites that provide general information about the rating. Also, as you would expect, if the rating gets downgraded the price of the bond could decrease. However, just because the bond rating changes, it doesn't mean necessarily that you should sell. In fact, as I said, the bond prices shouldn't cause you great concern as long as you are holding the bond to maturity. What's important is that the issuers make their interest payments to you, the investor.

Table 3 list the default rates as determined by Moody's investor services dated April 2007. The entire report can be viewed on Moody's website. It's clear that the better the rating the least likely that the bond issuers will default on making their interest payments. As the table shows, there is more than a 50% chance that the lowest rated bond will default in 5 years and conversely there is a .1% chance that a Aaa rated bond will default in 5 years and that there is less than a 2% chance that an investment grade bond will default.

Anyone can get access to this information and can research a bond on the Moody's website for free. They also have an enhanced service that can be purchased that provides extensive reports. All you have to know is the CUSIP or issuers name. The CUSIP is a number given to each bond offering.

Table 3: Moody's default probabilities.

Variability of Cumulative Default Rate Estimates

Rating	1-Year		3-Year		5-Year	
	Mean	Stdev	Mean	Stdev	Mean	Stdev
Aaa	0.00%	0.00%	0.00%	0.00%	0.10%	0.07%
Aa	0.01%	0.01%	0.04%	0.02%	0.18%	0.06%
A	0.02%	0.01%	0.22%	0.04%	0.47%	0.08%
Baa	0.18%	0.03%	0.93%	0.10%	1.94%	0.19%
Ba	1.20%	0.08%	5.57%	0.30%	10.21%	0.53%
B	5.23%	0.18%	17.04%	0.56%	26.79%	0.90%
Caa-C	19.47%	0.75%	39.73%	1.59%	52.66%	2.33%

As you can see now, the aforementioned information gives us plenty of reason to buy and hold individual bonds. If researched properly, they can provide a steady income with little worries. They can provide diversity, and they can provide a high rate of return, if the risk is properly analyzed.

Nearly all bonds are valued at a face value of $1000. There are other types of bonds, but the majorities are valued at $1000. That means if you buy one bond and the bond is priced at, what is referred to as par, then it will cost you $1000 plus a small brokerage fee. You will also have to pay the interest to the parties that you are buying the bond from, which has accrued from the last interest payment. In essence you receive this money back when you receive the next scheduled interest payment. Typically online brokerages will provide access to live bond searches. Sometimes they can be placed over the phone through your brokerage account. You can see the pricing of bonds similar to the stock market where stocks are priced. The prices however, because of many reasons mentioned, could be higher or lower than the par value of $1000. If the bond price is less than $1000, it is considered a discount. If the bond price is higher than $1000 is considered to be at a premium. When looking at the prices in a live bond search the price will be shown in hundreds of dollars. This is convention and tradition. In other words, if the price is $1000, then the listing will be $100. If the bond price is $950 than the listing will be $95. Just multiply the listing price times 10 and this will give you the real price of the bond.

The coupon rate of the bond is the interest rate paid by the issuer. This interest rate is fixed for the duration of the bond. Interest payments are made to the investor usually twice per year, every six months. Here is another important feature of the bonds. The interest rate payment is calculated on the face value or par value of the bond, not on the purchase price. This can be a tremendous advantage. As an example, if one buys a bond at a discount, say $900 and the interest rate (coupon rate) is 6%. The yearly income is $1000 times 6%, which equals $60. The payments will be made in 2 payments every six months of $30 each. Since you pay $900 for the bond, the rate of return would be calculated at $60 over $900, which equals 6.67%. **So if bonds are purchased at discount, the rate of return will be higher than the coupon rate.** If bonds are purchased at a premium, then the rate of return is less than the coupon rate.

There is still a further advantage to bonds when the bond matures. The maturity is the end of the life of the bond. It maybe 2 years, 5 years, even 30 years or more. The maturity date will be on the bond. As an example of December 2015. This means that on December 2015, the bond matures and the face value must be returned to the bondholder. Here's the added feature, if the bond is purchased at discount say $900, you receive $1000. That would be a $100 capital gain. So we have a double advantage in bonds, if purchased at discount. Of course there may be many reasons why the price is reduced, and one must evaluate the reason before purchasing.

Some bonds have a call feature. This means that the issuing agency could call the bond before it matures and pay off the bondholder. This is always spelled out in the details of the bond. However, if the bonds are called before maturity, they almost always pay off above par. In other words, if they call the bonds ahead of maturity, they pay extra, a great advantage; but of course, you have the inconvenience of having to invest the money in another entity.

In summary, bonds should be an important part of an investment portfolio. They can provide secure income and if researched properly can provide a high rate of return. A stock listed on a major exchange will have a ticker, for example, the ticker for General Electric is GE. A bond is listed by a combination of numbers and letters called the CUSIP. For example a CUSIP for a bond may look like 544566GF8.

A final example will show the potential return of a discounted bond.

Face value	$1000
Coupon	6%
Rating	BBB
Purchase price	$900
Maturity	12/15/2012

The interest payments are $1000 times 6%, which is $60, paid $30 every six months. Total interest payments over five years will be $300 and a capital gain of $100 will be realized when it matures. Total return of $400 for each $1000 bond over the five years equates to 8.9% per year ($80/$900), on average per year considering both interest and capital gains.

Section 4.2

Closed-end income funds

Closed-end funds are a good investment when trying to achieve a level of diversification. The shares are underwritten and sold on the secondary market similar to common stock. They generally have a portfolio that includes multiple assets. A closed-end fund would invest in multiple individual bonds. The prospectus would outline the specific details, for example, they may target investment grade corporate bonds. Each fund would have a different goal. Some may be domestic, some maybe international. Most of the funds provide steady income, often on a monthly basis. **They are a good investment for someone who needs to preserve capital and obtain high income.** But by nature they are considered a conservative investment and can be used to anchor a portfolio. Of course, before investing one should review the investment description and objectives. There are 693 closed-end funds that exist. It is possible to own more than one fund, but it is better to make sure the objectives do not overlap. For example, you might invest in a fund that targets US government bonds, and one that targets investment grade corporate bonds. The point is, make sure you have different objectives when purchasing multiple funds. When purchasing multiple funds, an overall plan can provide diversity, good income and preservation of capital.

Closed-end funds are similar to conventional mutual funds, in that each fund invests in multiple assets depending on the objective of the fund. Conventional mutual funds are called open-end funds and the shares are sold and redeemed directly by the fund. One important distinction however is the tax consequences of mutual funds. They distribute capital gains to each shareholder by reducing the number of shares equal to the capital gains. Since the shareholder sees no tangible increase at the time of the capital gains distributions, the tax consequences are paid on gains the shareholder does not realize. The shareholder can recover the lost capital gains by reducing the cost basis when selling the shares. Unfortunately, it is very difficult to reconstruct these records, and in fact, most shareholders do not properly cost and recover the gains, but will usually use the purchase price of the original shares when calculating cost basis for tax purposes. Mutual funds that are open-end, for tax consequences are confusing, and their use is better served in portfolios that are in a tax-deferred account such as in IRA or 401.

The closed-end funds use a different method when calculating tax consequences. Income that is delivered (usually monthly) may be from either ordinary income, capital gains are both. At the end of the year the exact breakdown is given for your tax returns. This is a much cleaner way than the mutual funds. In short, for closed-end funds, one pays taxes on realized income and gain and doesn't pay taxes on money you don't see.

The second important feature of the closed-end funds over the conventional open-ended mutual funds is that since they are sold on the open market, the purchase price could be above or below the net asset value. The NAV is the total assets divided by the number of shares outstanding. The conventional open-end mutual fund is always priced at the end of the trading day at the net asset value. Since the shares of the closed-end funds are sold on the open market, the prices are somewhat market-driven. Therefore a very important factor when buying closed-end funds is to review its net asset value. When buying below the net asset value it is considered to be at discount, and vice versa, when buying above the NAV, it is considered to be at a premium. Of course, it is desirable to buy at a discount, but one should review the history of the pricing to determine the reason. If everything appears solid financially, than buying at a discount can be very lucrative and would improve the total return on the investment. Another factor that should be considered before buying is the fee structure. Look for low expense ratios and funds that do not charge upfront or redemption fees. There are many good closed-end funds that have no fees and very low expenses. I have paid attention to this, and have found no studies that have shown a better return for a loaded fund (a fund that charges a fee upfront to invest).

In summary, close-end funds can provide, worry free income over many years if reviewed properly upfront. Very little work is required periodically. More importantly, they provide an anchoring element in your portfolio. It's important to have some assets that protect your capital; in addition, they can provide a high level of income. Since income could be from capital gains or ordinary income, this can provide a beneficial tax advantage. However, like most other investments, not all closed-end funds are the same. Some may use leverage to increase returns. This is not necessarily bad. The good story overall is that a review of the few aforementioned parameters will lead to an easy decision to purchase or to pass.

Section 4.3

Certificates of deposits (CD's)

Nearly everyone is familiar with CD's. Generally they are issued by local banks and savings and loans. In addition, since deregulation, much other type of institutions offers CD's. They may seem very bland and are overlooked by many investors. They still have a following with seniors. I think they should and could be part of anyone's portfolio plan. They have a tremendous amount of safety because they are backed by insurance from the Federal Depository Insurance Corporation or FDIC. Each account is guaranteed up to $125,000 by the government. This was a feature added as a result of the stock market crash of 1929. It was one of many comprehensive actions that stabilized the banking industry and the economy.

Interest rates are usually higher when the maturity is longer. Most of the time there are penalties for removing the money before maturity. Each entity that issues the CD's set their own rules; make sure you ask specifics before investing in CD's. **Since they are insured, they're typically an investment that protects your capital and provides some income.** Interest rates, or return, are not considered to be high, but the return is considered secondary.

Sometimes it may be useful to ladder the CD investments. A ladder may be built by buying CD's with various maturities, possibly maturity every one year. As an example, one might purchase CD's with a maturity of one year, two-year, three year, and four years. What that means, is that each year the principal would be available for new investments. It would be more desirable to use a ladder when interest rates are on the rise. It's probably not a very good idea to purchase CD's greater than four years, except in high interest rate environments. If interest rates are high and possibly peaking, it may be beneficial to buy long-term maturity CD's.

In summary, CD's should be considered in a well-planned portfolio. They provide a great advantage of protecting capital but usually the low risk equates to an average return. **However keep in mind, that a low return in all cases is better than a negative return and possibly the loss of capital.**

Section 4.4

Government EE and I savings bonds

Government EE saving bonds were the first investment vehicle that I became familiar with. It taught me the important aspects of investing; giving up resources and getting a return. EE saving bonds are still a good way for young people to get involved in investing. Birthday and Christmas money could be used to purchase savings bonds. Having resources as a young person can be a great learning experience. Some companies offer savings bonds in their 401(k) s savings plans. Even though, generally the interest rates are lower, they are a very secure investment, since they are backed by the good faith of the US government. They also support the operation of the government, but EE bonds should be invested, primarily for their security.

They also have a very tangible feeling, similar to money. You actually get a piece of paper that shows the details of the bond. It gives the date of purchase and the denomination (face value). It is thicker than money and has the feel of thin cardboard. It's similar to the old punch cards that were used in the early days of computers. I believe this unique aspect also helps young people feel connected to their investments. I know I got a kick out of feeling and looking at the green bonds. The bonds are numbered and have issue dates. This information should be recorded for safekeeping in case they get lost.

Nearly all other investments are on paper or electronic and quite remote from the investor. Some banks still have a passbook which log deposits and withdraws. This was the primary investments for money for many people for many years. One would open the passbook to see how much money they had. EE savings bonds are still available and are usually

mailed to the purchaser. It's not clear how long the
government will continue to issue the bonds.

EE savings bonds are issued at 50% of the face value.
That means a bond issued at $100, costs only $50. It is offered
in eight denominations, $50, $75, $100, $200, $500, $1000,
$5,000 and $10,000. There is an annual $30,000 face value
limit per person. The $25 face value bond has been eliminated.
The interest is calculated as 90% of the six month averages of
the five-year treasury yields. The interest rates are announced
every six months, May 1 and September 1. The interest rate
will be fixed for the life of the bond. The savings bonds are
not exactly like other bonds, in fact, there is not a maturity
date. The bonds may be cashed any time after 1 year. If cashed
within five years, there is a three-month interest penalty. This
is another advantage of the bonds; they are really liquid,
meaning you can instantly cash them at most banks. The
interest will start accruing on a monthly basis compounded
semiannually. However it is guaranteed to reach face value at
a maximum of 17 years. The interest earned on the bond is
considered tax-deferred and will not be paid until the bond is
redeemed. This method is quite different from ordinary bonds.
See chapter on bonds for methods of other bonds (Section 4.1).
The bonds can be held for 30 years and interest will continue to
build until that time. After 30 years the interest will stop
occurring. You can determine the present value of your bonds
by going to the bond calculator on their website. The exact link
is given in a later chapter.

If young people purchase EE savings bonds from their
birthday and Christmas monies and then cashed them before
they incur a job, and have little substantial income, then for the
most part, the money earned will be tax-free. The minimum
income before paying income tax changes each year and
therefore should be reviewed. The bonds must be issued with
their Social Security numbers. The bonds still provide a great
advantage to all other investments because the bond interest is

not taxed until cashed in, and they may be cashed in, at the owner's discretion. Also if used for educational purposes, it could be tax exempt under most circumstances. Once again tax law changes and should be reviewed.

The government has now introduced a new savings bond similar to the EE, called I bonds. They do have some distinct differences. They are issued at face value, meaning it costs $100, for $100 bond. The biggest difference is that the interest rate, instead of having a fixed interest rate for the life of the bond, the interest rate has both a fixed and variable component. The variable rate is added to a base fixed rate which is calculated based on the Consumer Price Index (CPI). In essence, one gets an inflation protected rate of return when purchasing I bonds. Of course, no one knows what will happen to interest rates over the life of the bond. **If interest rates go down during the period of the bond, it would be better to buy EE bonds, if interest rates go up during that period, it would be better to buy I bonds.** If you feel that inflation could pop its ugly head, then I bonds is the safer bet. The longer the bonds are held, the more you would want to lean towards the I bonds. All other features of I bonds are the same as EE bonds.

So savings bonds are not just for young people, they can provide exceedingly secure income, provide a level of return, and are very flexible concerning the tax consequences. Savings bonds are also a good place to start an investment portfolio. It one never invested in any other vehicle, and then savings bonds are a good place to start. They can be purchased online from the treasury department or simply go to your local bank or savings and loan. In all cases the bonds will be mailed to your home. So heck, go out and buy a savings bond today.

Section 4.5

Treasury securities

To support the public debt, the US government asks citizens like you and me to provide our resources. There are many vehicles that are available to small and large investors. Since the US government has one of the strongest and most stable economies in the world, likewise their investments are also considered to be the most secure. In fact, all other investments are graded against the US government returns. Treasury bills are the safest but usually have the lowest rate of returns. It is considered a base rate of return, sometimes referred to as a benchmark, in that risk and return for all other investments are higher. The US treasury yield curve establishes interest rates usually up to 30 years. So if you want to see how your investments are doing, check the treasury yield curve. The Yield curve can be viewed on a daily basis and it changes on a daily basis. The best place to view the curve is Bloomberg's website, which I have included the link in a later chapter. The graph always shows the present and day before rates. Graph 3 shows that the curve looks a little funky right now. Normally, the 3 and 6 month rate would be much lower. This funny yield curve could be telling us something. As you can see the short term and long term rates are very close.

Graph 2. Treasury Yield Curve

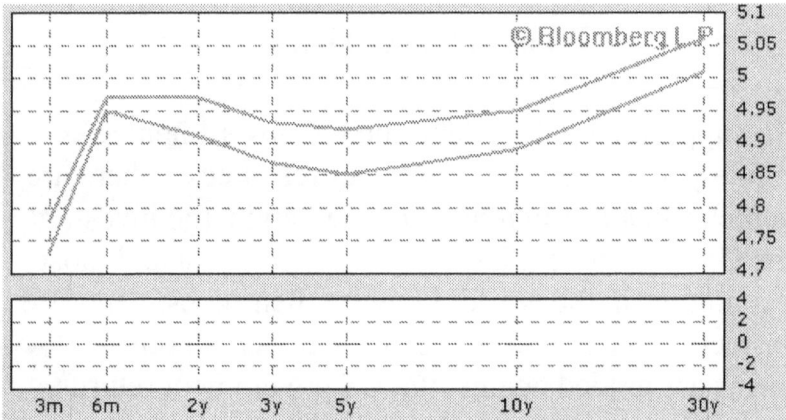

Graph 3 shows the yield curve as of June 2, 2007. Treasury securities fall into many categories; some include T-bills, notes and bonds. The yield curve consists of the 3 and 6 month T-bill and the 2, 3,5,10 and 30 year bond rates. T-bills and notes/bonds can be purchased in open markets. This means that the price fluctuates similar to stock prices. They are liquid and can be bought and sold easily. The best place to purchase is the treasury direct website. They do not issue paper like they do for savings bonds; therefore your balances and transactions are generally kept online.

In summary, Government T-bills and notes are the securest investments one can find. Some investments in everyone's portfolio must come from secure investments; this could fit the "bill" for some investors. It is considered a no worry, risk-free investment. Sometimes it's easier to invest in government bond funds. This could come in the form of a closed-end or open-end income fund. In some cases it may be simpler and provide the same security and worry free investments. However keep in mind your return would be slightly lower than it would be if you had invested directly in the instruments since investment fees in funds could reduce your return. Never overlook a good T-bill.

Section 4.6

Preferred stocks

Preferred stocks are a unique type of security. You might say that they are a cross between a common stock and a bond. Some companies have offerings where they sell a category of stock they call preferred. It's preferred only in the sense that it has closer ties to the assets of the company. See chapter on liquidation rights. It has a little lesser rights than company bonds but more rights than common stock. The shares of preferred stock also give a dividend. The dividend is usually stipulated and if everything goes well for the company, they will continue to pay a dividend. Most often the share par value is set at $25, or sometimes multiples like $50, or $100, but usually $25. The shares after issue is sold on the open market, so like a share of common stock, the price can fluctuate. If the shares are priced below the par, $25, then the purchaser will buy at discount and the return will be greater than the established rate. If the shares are purchased for greater than par, $25, then the rate of return will be reduced. Most often the preferred stock, just like bonds have a maturity date, at which the company will reimburse the holder, the par value of $25. Some preferred stocks have an open call date and may be called, whenever, at the company's discretion. It is considered a conservative investment since it is higher on liquidation poll than common stock and somewhat guarantees a return. Some companies have issued preferred shares many years ago and continue to pay dividends; in fact, it's not required that they have a maturity date. As one can expect, preferred stock price is tied very closely to the interest rate that is affixed to the share. Therefore the stock price will not deviate very far from the par, $25. As the price starts to creep above $25, the reduced return will hold further increases in stock price. Likewise as the price reduces the return will increase to the point that the market will bring in more buyers. **This inherent basic principle of preferred stock gives a very stable unit price with a high level of security for providing income.** Like any other investment, it's important to research the investments before investing.

In summary, preferred stocks can be another solid investment that gives a great income, and if properly analyzed a low risk. If you are looking for a stable investment, and it fits in your plan, then preferred stocks could be for you.

Section 4.7

Dividend paying stocks

Common stocks paid dividends in the early years of the stock market. The original idea was to have everybody and anybody take part in the capitalization of America. In fact until the 1960's most stocks paid some dividend. The speculation in the stock market began to be more prevalent after the 1980's. In my mind, it's not a bad thing to own common stocks that don't pay a dividend, but the real problem becomes, what are they worth.

Unfortunately the only real indicator of what a stock is worth is what somebody will pay for it. Since there is really no exact calculation one can use, all sorts of technical valuations come into play. Price to earnings (P/E), five-year sales growth, number one or number two in market share, really the list is endless and fruitless to continue. None of these or any other indicator will give an exact value to what a stock is worth. However, a stock that has dividends will trade in a controlled range. As soon as the dividends are raised, it is pretty absolute that the share price will likewise rise. Consider a stock when the dividend is reduced, it is pretty absolute that the stock price will go down. There is no other indicator that has as close a correlation to stock price as the dividend. If one is following a stock that pays a regular dividend, forget all other indicators that most stock pickers review. **It can therefore be asserted that it is much more secure and manageable if one follows an investment stock that pays dividends.** Of course not all stocks that pay dividends are a good buy and should be purchased. Company strategies and resources must still be analyzed to convince oneself that going forward; the company is capable of continuing the dividend. Track record is a good indicator. If a company has been paying dividends and may even have been increasing those dividends, it is a better choice, everything being equal.

As an example, take General Electric, GE. GE has been paying dividends each quarter for over 100 years. In addition, GE's dividends have been raised, 31 consecutive years. This is an absolutely astonishing record. It has settled over many years into about a 2.5% dividend. That means it pays 2.5% of the stock price as a cash payout. Anybody that follows GE knows that the company will continue paying a 2.5% dividend, unless some catastrophic problem occurs. You can check the stock price, if the yield it above 2.5% then it's probably a good time to buy. It's no surprise that the stock price appreciation has increased with the dividend increases.

There are other common stocks that have paid dividends for many years with similar stories. Even though they pay dividends, they still are considered growth stocks and in many cases have outpaced the average growth rates. It's worth searching out the long-term dividend payers and considering an investment.

So how long should a stock have been paying a dividend to have been considered to have a good track record? I like to use a five-year span. Of course longer is even better. It's really up to the investor, and the investment. Some track records may be able to be established in three years, some track records may not be able to be established for 10 years. It's important to look at their track record and make a decision as to how comfortable you are with this investment.

Another indicator that can be used to judge the capability of the entity to continue paying dividends is the payout ratio. The payout ratio is usually in a percentage and gives the amount of income used to pay out dividends. For example if a company uses 50% of its income, i.e. 50% payout ratio, then there is a high probability that the company can continue to pay dividends. If a company has a payout ratio of 110% then this indicates the company may be having problems paying its dividends and future dividends may be at risk. Another indicator that I like to review before buying a common stock that pays a dividend is the history of the dividends. Have the dividends risen consistently or have they been decreasing or have they been going up and down. Once again, this would be a good indicator showing the stability of the company. Obviously, rising dividends are more beneficial.

The argument against stocks that pay a dividend stem around the idea of speculation. The large swings of stock prices usually will occur with stocks that do not pay dividends. This indicator is called the beta of a stock. A high beta indicates that the stock price moves wildly. A low beta indicates that the stock price varies little. Stocks that pay dividends generally have a low beta. This is the knock against dividend paying stocks. If one is speculating on the price appreciation then it's a better bet to go with a stock that has a track record of high price movements. The tricky part of dealing with these types of stocks is that they can also go down wildly. So the problem with buying and selling stocks is that you have to time your orders correctly to make money. And the problem is that it requires constant review and awareness of changes or milestones. Some people enjoy this type of investing, which can be exciting and of course if you make the right call, can be financially rewarding. Likewise they can be financially disastrous if the call is wrong. **It seems eminently clear that there is a place and time for speculating on common stocks that don't pay a dividend.** There seems to be an inborn desire to make the big score. Doubling your money in a short period of time can be exhilarating.

It seems like the place for these types of investments is when you already have your portfolio protected. Take 10 or 15% of your portfolio and look for that great stock and speculate. Play your hunches or get that stock tip but don't gamble away your future security. Be disciplined and only command a small portion of your portfolio. It's not a good idea to spend $5000 or $10,000 on a stock if you only have $20,000 in your portfolio.

In summary, stocks that pay dividends bring a nice mix to anyone's portfolio. They can provide constant income and if they have a history of increasing dividends, they can be considered a growth stock that will add to your increasing wealth. Stocks that do not pay dividends should be invested with a small portion of your wealth. **The price of a stock is directly tied to the dividend and will move as the dividend moves.** Stocks that pay dividends come from all sectors of the economy. Don't overlook the fact that a stock may pay a dividend, use this to your advantage.

Section 4.8

Real estate investment trusts (REITS)

REIT's are a corporate entity that issues shares of stock and then uses the proceeds to purchase real estate assets or in

some cases mortgage assets tied to real estate. The shares are
then traded on the open market like common stock shares.
Nearly all REIT's pay a dividend based on the efficiency of the
investments. REIT's have a unique tax methodology in that
the entities that issue the shares do not pay taxes on income,
but the tax consequences are passed to the holder of the shares
as long as they meet certain requirements. Generally the REIT
entity must pass on a minimum of approximately 90% of its
income. Since the REIT entity only keeps around 10% of its
profits, it is not in a position to grow its assets. Generally the
REIT entity will issue new shares to generate new income,
which could have a dilution effect on the existing shares, but if
the company has a good track record, then additional
investments could increase its return. They also have the
opportunity to sell existing assets to reestablish new
investments. Therefore the price of the shares has some
opportunity for growth, although it's not considered a growth
investment, generally, but usually have a fairly high income
return. REIT's generally invest their assets in one real estate
sector, such as, office buildings, apartments, shopping centers,
health care centers, restaurants, hotels, etc. This means that the
REIT industry is not monolithic since not all real estate sectors
follow suit. This type of investment requires more research
than the investments in the previous sections. Some real estate
sectors could be cyclical and therefore the dividends could
fluctuate with the happenings of the sector. For example,
occupancy rates of buildings for a sector could diminish to the
point where dividends are reduced. Since the dividends are
tied to the stock price, if the dividends get reduced, so goes the
stock price. If in fact, some REITs get in trouble, they would
provide a very minimal dividend, which would put tremendous
pressure on the stock price. When looking at REIT's, consider
entities that have a good track record. I would consider REIT's
that have provided stable returns for at least five years. One
should also review projects that they have, what markets do

they serve, et cetera.

When reviewing the objectives of a REIT, it is very important to distinguish the assets that are being held. Some REIT's invests in the real estate itself, meaning that it owns properties. Some other REIT's hold the mortgages and loans associated with properties. The latter is a more risky investment. Although they generally have higher returns, they are subject to interest rate movements and therefore their stock price will be somewhat very volatile. If interest rates are moving down, then it is not uncommon to see these types of REIT's move substantially down in stock price. This is so because they are making their money on the loans, not the operation of the real estate. **Sticking with REIT's that own property is a safer way to go, rather than those REIT's that hold loans on properties, until you have understood the nuances of this type of investment.**

There are also available open and close-end funds that invest in multiple REIT's. Mutual funds for REIT's could provide a more diversified investment. Remember that when purchasing mutual funds, the fees will reduce your total return. Also, as I stated in the closed-end section (4.2), closed-end funds have advantages over open-end funds (mutual funds).

In summary, REIT's can provide a great income and good diversification to your portfolio. There are 193 different REIT's available for investment. They require a little more research than other fixed income investments. **Overall, real estate provides many advantages to an investor and REIT's are a great means for the small investor to get a piece of this industry.** They can be a fun investment. You have the opportunity to actually visit your buildings, see where your resources are going, and where your income is coming from. So if it fits in your plan, take a look at REIT's.

Section 4.9

Master limited partnerships (MLP's)

A much overlooked investment vehicle is the MLP. Probably because they are a little confusing and not covered by a majority of the analyst. However they have more advantages than any other investment vehicle.

MLPs are Master limited partnerships that were set up by Congress in the early 1980s for the purpose of oil and energy exploration and research. Therefore the majority of MLPs is in the energy field but is not limited to energy. Most of the oil and natural gas pipelines are set up as MLPs. They pay no taxes and pass along both income and deductions to the shareholder, or in this case, limited partners. The shares of an MLP are called units. A general partner runs the partnership and collects a fee. The majority of income is then passed on to the unit holders, often as a monthly or quarterly distribution. Since they are not followed by a lot of investors, the return is quite high. Here is the great part of MLPs. They can truly be called a tax shelter because the cost of business, including capital equipment depreciation is also passed on to the investor. Pipelines and oil equipment are very expensive; therefore the depreciation deductions are hefty. **So the income that is distributed to the limited partners are mostly offset by deductions, which means the income realistically is tax-deferred until you sell the units or could even be tax-free.**

One downside to MLP's is the tax records that are required for filing. MLPs are required to send out a K-1 tax form with the details of income and deductions. Also they are not required to mail the form until March. This could be a disadvantage since you have to file your tax return by April 15. If one uses a software program like TurboTax, the forms can usually be downloaded directly from the MLPs website into the tax software. Like REITs, MLPs have the potential to deliver high income, and growth. Also like REITs, MLPs usually sell additional units to add capacity, expand capabilities or improve performance. This could dilute shares if the additional resources do not come to fruition and could eventually reduce the distribution. However with energy and particular oil and natural gas prices on the rise, the distribution seems to be solid for years to come. Like other investments that pay dividends, the unit prices are usually stable. This low volatility makes them a very conservative investment. If one is willing to work through the tax forms, the investor will get great rewards. **Like any other energy asset, as oil becomes more and more depleted, MLPs will be more valuable.**

The yields for MLPs have ranged between three and four points above treasury yields. It appears to be a great reward for the risk concerning most MLPs. The risks seem to be no greater than other energy stocks, but pipelines for instance do provide an easy target for those waiting to do harm. This could provide some additional risk. Also since the world oil reserves are reaching a peak over the next few years, the cost of oil and natural gas prices will escalate and could become very volatile as demand starts to exceed capacity. It's uncertain how this problem will exactly play out.

It seems however, in summary, that the benefits and advantages of owning MLPs thoroughly outweigh the inconvenience of working through the tax forms and the risk. One can expect from MLPs a high rate of return, a high growth potential, and a tax shelter advantage. MLPs have a truly triple whammy of greatness, so go ahead, if it fits in your plan, do your homework and become a limited partner.

Section 4.10

Royalty trusts

Royalty Trusts have to be the biggest hidden investment vehicle known to mankind. This class of investment seems to get very little play in financial magazines, newspapers or financial periodicals.

There are approximately 24 royalty trusts in the United States that are available for investment. They were established as a financial vehicle to distribute royalties or profits from a particular asset. Most of the royalty trusts have assets in energy, mostly oil and natural gas. These are not stocks in oil companies. Oil company stocks return very little of their profits over to the stock holder. Royalty Trusts are a way to get in on the profits in oil. The trusts are usually administered by a bank or financial institution trustee. They are required to distribute virtually all of the income made from the assets. Royalty Trusts are sold on the exchanges similar to common stock. They are great vehicle for producing income. **Royalty Trusts generally have a very high rate of return, four to six points above the treasury rates, at least.** When first evaluating the royalty trust class of investments they seem to be too good to be true, since they return a high level of income.

However, there are some disadvantages or one may say pitfalls when investing in royalty trusts. The dividends are usually distributed monthly but sometimes quarterly. As I said, all of the income, from the last payout is distributed to the investor minus any maintenance or administration costs. If for example, the assets are oil wells, the income will be based on the price of oil at that time. So in this case, the dividends will be reflective of the price of a barrel of oil. When oil is high, the dividends will be high, when oil is low, the dividends will be lower. Another risk associated with royalty trust is the fact that the assets usually have a limited life. For instance if a trust is set up to manage a particular oil well and that oil well begins to deplete its reserves, thereby causing the output production to decrease, then the dividends will also be reduced, reflective of the output production. This makes the royalty trust investment a very difficult investment to analyze and it is somewhat difficult to foretell what the dividend will be in the future. However, if one is able to live with a roller coaster dividend and willing to accept a limited life for that dividend, then royalty trusts can provide a very high rate of return. **A key point in analyzing oil royalty reserves is the depletion timetables.** The prospectus will show the number of years the oil well is expected to produce. Keep in mind oil depletion figures change yearly, that is to say oil depletion projections are constantly changing. Some investors may not feel comfortable with this uncertainty, yes for sure, royalty trusts have many uncertainties.

In summary, royalty trusts can provide a very high level of income, in addition, if the underlying assets of the royalty trusts are in demand, stock price appreciation at a very high level can occur. It requires an extensive amount of research before investing in royalty trust, but don't let a little work stop you from obtaining profits from the oil industry, if it fits in your plan.

Section 4.11

Business development companies (BDC's)

What do these three companies have in common? Piper aircraft, Bumblebee tuna, and Bushnell optics. If you guessed that they are private companies, then you are correct. This is just three of thousands of private corporations in the United States that operate in our economy. However, up until 1980 it was nearly impossible for the small investor to be able to invest in these types of entities. Therefore, in 1980 Congress created regulation to encourage the flow of public resources into private businesses. This of course, was a new opportunity for small and individual investors to obtain profits from many of the small companies that exist in our economy. Of course, everyone has the capabilities of investing in public corporations through common stock and bond offerings. Since 1980 there have been 25 companies, called business development companies (BDC's), dedicated to providing resources to small and medium companies. The BDC's funnel money to these private entities through stock offerings and financial institution loans. The stock of the BCD trades on exchanges similar to common stock. It is a great way for the small investor to get a piece of private enterprises. Usually a BDC will invest in many small companies, thereby diversifying its risk. The returns are usually paid quarterly and are above average as compared to common stock dividends. It's quite common for a BDC to have provided resources to as many as 50 to 100 different entities. Once again the track record of the BDC is a very important indicator as to the capabilities and resources the company has developed. Every outstanding loan they have made is available for review. Some of the BDC's have established track records more than 10 years. This should give a potential investor a good indication as to what level of dividend can be expected in the future. Since there exist only 25 BDC's, it is fairly straightforward to analyze and reduce the field.

In summary, BDC's can provide a high level of income and good growth potential for the stock price. They are fairly easy to evaluate since that the track record is available. A list of the companies, that the BDC provide loans to, is available to the investor before purchasing shares. Of course, the most important parameter that an income investor is concerned about is the dividend. Go ahead, if it fits in your plan, get your piece of the pie in private financing, and select a BDC.

Section 4.12

Stock options

Every investor knows about options. They have heard the term, but very few have actually been an investor in stock options. Stock options that are traded on the open market are quite different than the company stock options that are given out by some companies to employees. Some companies give employees as an incentive to good performance, free options on their stock, meaning they can sell and keep the difference between a stock selling price and the option price. So when a stock increases in price, this incentive becomes more valuable. However, stock options that are sold in the open markets have nothing to do with these company stock options.

The stock options I'm talking about are bought and sold as an entity unto themselves. I may surprise you in these next statements. What investment has less risk than US government securities? What investment has a 100% guaranteed return? What investment has a zero chance of failing? Have you given up yet? Most people do not believe this type of investment exists, but it does. It's called a covered option call. Sometimes referred to as a covered call. That's right a covered call option is a 100% guaranteed investment. You are positively guaranteed to get a return. In fact, the exact moment that you press the sell button, you receive your return. It instantly gets credited to your account. It's your money instantly!

So now that you understand that a covered call is a guaranteed investment, how does one invest in a covered call?

Think of a call option as the right to buy or sell shares of a stock. For example, if you already own 100 shares of a company, say XYZ, then you have the right to sell a call option on your shares. Each option contract is 100 shares of the stock. The option price is the amount you are willing to sell your option. Another person, may be willing to buy your call option for the price you are willing to sell it for. If this becomes a mutual agreement, similar to normal stock trading, then the option contract is sold by you and bought by another party for the agreed-upon price. Remember you're not actually selling your 100 shares at this point; you are selling the right to those 100 shares. If your share price is at $50 at the time you sell your call option and the option price is one dollar, then you are selling the rights to your shares at $51. This means that if the price approaches $51, the other party that bought your option has the right to purchase your shares. You have no claim on the shares after the price reaches $51. If the price goes to $55, you've not gotten the $4 benefit above $51. The party that bought the option has the right to purchase your shares at $51 and then sell at $55. They would then receive the $4 benefit. Giving them a $4 return on the $1 investment they made. So in this transaction you made $1 and the party buying the option made $4 when the price went to $55. Nobody losses, you just don't gain as much as you would if you would have passed on the option. On the flip side you have guaranteed yourself a $1 profit. On the other hand, if the price does not move above $50 or goes lower, you will continue to hold your stock, and of course, you will always keep the $1 option price. The party buying your one dollar call option loses 100% of their money with $0 return. The one additional factor is that your option call that you sold has a finite time. If your stock hasn't been purchased by the date on the option, it will expire and the right to your stock goes away. You can sell your options usually 1-8months out. So when you sell covered option calls you are getting instant cash at the option price. It goes into your account and you are able to use the money. What you are giving up is the potential upside to your stock above the option price. You can think of it this way, you're getting some of the upside potential immediately but giving up any additional gains above the option price during the duration of the option. As you can see there is no risk on this investment. But be aware and listen intently, investing in all other forms of options are risky and you should be experienced before investing. Options are traded through an online brokerage and one needs to get approval before investing in options. In fact there are multiple levels of approvals. The first level approval for options is for covered calls only. After investing and understanding options, additional approvals can be utilized to buy calls, and to buy and sell puts. I'm not going to tell you about putts. The intention for this article is to introduce the idea of covered calls. Further information is necessary before investing in other type of options.

In summary, covered call options can provide instant cash and can be a rewarding and profitable investing vehicle. Take the time to research the mechanics of options and only sign up for covered call approval. You cannot get hurt or make stupid mistakes. **Covered calls are a 100% guaranteed investment.** All other investments in options can be risky and should be performed by experienced people. So if you need some instant money and are willing to give up some upside potential to a stock that you presently hold, and it fits in your plan, consider covered call options.

Chapter 5

Liquidation preference

So far just about everything you have read in this book up to now has been very positive. I've been giving a very upbeat picture of investing. Unfortunately, now is the time to present the downside of investing. The day will come in every investor's life where one of their investments goes belly up. It's important to understand what will happen when one or more of your entities go into bankruptcy proceedings. In fact, the more you understand the process before hand, the more you can protect yourself from total disaster.

So here is what happens. The company you've invested in starts having difficulties, they get over extended, default on their bonds and decide that filing for bankruptcy is their only option. If it's hopeless they immediately file chapter 7 and dissolve, if they want to continue, they file chapter 11 or 13 and reorganize. What does this mean to you as the investor? Will you lose everything? The answer to that question depends on what kind of security in the company you are holding. Are you a creditor i.e. bond holder or are you a passive investor (unsecured) holding common stock.

If the company goes totally bankrupt (chapter 7) and decides to shut down the company and dissolve all assets, then typically the assets will be distributed based on, what is called, the liquidation preference. The court will appoint someone, sometimes called a liquidator, to carry out the liquidation of the company's assets. The following list gives a basic view of this preference.

<u>Priority of claims for liquidation purposes</u>

1. Secured creditors or creditors with liens
2. Costs of liquidation- this could also be a creditor.
3. Preferred creditors.
4. Unsecured creditors.

In essence, those creditors higher on the list will get paid first. Of course, the government gets paid first, any outstanding taxes or levies. If there is anything left, then secured bondholders will get paid. If after secured bondholders are paid then assets will be distributed to preferred stock holders, then if anything is left, assets will be distributed to common stock holders. So when reviewing the assets of the company one may be able to determine how far up the food

chain the assets will take you if liquidation occurs. Generally, as you probably expect, very rarely do common stockholders ever get anything. Also not all bonds are the same, some maybe secured and some may be a different class. It pays to look for the type of bond or stock you are buying in case of liquidation. It should say secured, preferred or unsecured.

A lot of times the stock prices goes lower and lower as the process takes place. It may be a good buy, sometimes reducing to less than one dollar per share. You can really load up, but be aware, even if the company news reports indicate positive information; this is a very risky investment. There are some investment companies that play these very cheap stocks where the company is in financial straits. They usually buy large amounts but are only looking for pennies in stock price movement. It's not uncommon for a $.20 stock to move five cents plus or minus. If they purchase hundreds of thousands of shares, they can make a lot of money on a five cent price increase. Anyway the moral is, you have to be a very sophisticated and knowledgeable investor to get into a stock that is in bankruptcy.

So you can see, if you hold a company secured bond, you have a reasonably good chance of getting some money back. This is another advantage to holding bonds in your portfolio. This gives them another reason to be considered a secure investment.

Now I need to further explain and show how this downside to investing gets even lower. The list I have shown are used for liquidation preferences, meaning if the company goes out of business. Unfortunately for you as an investor, most companies don't liquidate. I really mean it when I say, unfortunately for you as an investor. I don't mean any ill will to employees, customers or other creditors. I'm sure a lot of lives are hurt when companies close their doors. I'm purely looking at this from an investor point of view. You, as the investor, would receive, in most cases, far more assets if the company were to simply liquidate its assets. I can't always make that claim, because some companies are very generous to their investors, but most are not.

So what really happens is that companies exit bankruptcy chapter (11 or 13) still operating their businesses, but with less debt. It has become a sorry state of affairs for investors over the past few years. Most bankruptcy courts have favored the companies and have allowed them to reduce their debt burden on the backs of investors. It has become a management tactic rather than a happening of last resort. I can show you many, many company statements that have "bragged" about exiting bankruptcy with a lower debt burden.

So if you are holding bonds from a company that goes into bankruptcy, you could have several possible outcomes.

1.) Interest coupon rate reduced.
2.) Number of bonds you hold reduced.
3.) Bonds terminated and exchanged for stock.
4.) Bonds exchanged for reduced cash value.
5.) Receive nothing.
6.) Any combination of the above.

Remember if the company liquidates, you will get your fair share of the assets, however if the company exits bankruptcy court, the court will determine what the creditors (you) will get. Of course, you as the creditor have voting rights and you will be asked to approve the outcome. Usually the small investor has very little clout in trying to affect the outcome. I have owned bonds that went to bankruptcy where income funds owned the same bond and were able to use some leverage to get the output increased. This isn't usually the case. In my many years of investing, I have had all five of the above outcomes and more, basically you never know what to expect out of bankruptcy. The only thing for certain is that you will get less than what you started with.

I'd like to share an experience I had concerning a bankruptcy court. I am happy to report that this is one of few examples where I've felt I was fairly treated in a bankruptcy court. As many of you know, Donald Trump operates casinos in Atlantic City. Some of you may also consider him to be a ruthless businessman. But my experience and tiny association proved differently. The Donald financed, in part, his casino activity utilizing corporate bonds. I purchased several of those bonds as an investment vehicle. The first few years went by as planned, where I collected my interest payments on schedule. Then the bomb was dropped, Trump Casino Resorts were having difficulties and defaulted on paying the bond interest. They went into bankruptcy and eventually exited bankruptcy. Out of the bankruptcy proceedings, I received new bonds issued at a reduced interest rate and company common stock. The number of bonds was fewer than I had going in, but the value of the combination of new bonds and common stock was very similar to the value, and my investment, as the original bonds. The proceedings went very quickly, less than a year. I did lose an interest payment, but I was even compensated for some unpaid interest after exiting bankruptcy. I have to say, I was very pleased with this outcome. I lost very little and Trump Resorts became financially stronger. I don't know what will happen in the future, but at this point, things are going well, I'm receiving my interest payments and the common stock is doing well. I have to compliment Donald Trump for treating the smalltime investor, like myself very fairly. Of course, I don't know the background and details that precipitated this fair arrangement. I have had several other bond holdings go into bankruptcy and never had this kind of results. Thank you Donald.

The other bad thing is that this process can take years. I literally mean years. The entity will first default on its interest payment then at some point declares bankruptcy. That means your money is tied up and you are not making any return.

Even if you end up getting a payout, you have lost the interest payments while in bankruptcy. I have had bonds in bankruptcy for over four years. I know it sounds almost ridiculous, but it's true. Expect at least one maybe two years before you hear anything. I held bonds in a company, that exited bankruptcy, where I received zilch, but it took two years to complete the action of the court, so to add insult to injury, I couldn't even deduct the loss on my income taxes for those two years because the lawyers had not executed the court outcome. As you probably can guess, bankruptcy can be a very frustrating and expensive proposition to you as an investor. The best way to avoid this process is to do your homework when selecting your investments, and select lower risk investments. See Bond default ratings section 4.1. Even if you do everything correctly, if you invest long enough, you will have investments that go into bankruptcy. When that happens, don't get stressed out. If you have a good plan in place, it won't hurt your overall picture. Just consider it, the cost of doing business, and remember, you get some of your losses returned by taking a tax deduction.

I have one more piece of information that I would like to share concerning bankruptcy proceedings. Often times when a company declares bankruptcy, it doesn't have the necessary resources to continue operation. Nearly all bankruptcy courts allow the entity in bankruptcy, to take out a loan to continue its operation during the bankruptcy proceedings. Number 2 on the liquidation preference list was cost of liquidation, or in this case, reorganization. This means that a company has not been able to adequately handle its finances, but the courts are allowing them to take an additional loan to complete the bankruptcy proceedings. You probably know where I'm going with this; these loans are always on the top of the liquidation preference (number 2). This means that they will be paid ahead of, some existing bondholders (creditors). This is another slap in the face to existing investors. This new loan will be paid off, even though you may get nothing out of the bankruptcy court.   The only good news here is that you can invest in those companies that are supplying these new loans to corporations in bankruptcy. So look around, you have the opportunity to get your piece of the loans that corporations are using to proceed through bankruptcy. Sometimes they are called bridge or mezzanine loans.

The bottom line, just keep this process in mind when you select your investments. It should not give you paralysis when investing; it's just another aspect and parameter to help you tailor a long term investment plan.

Chapter 6

Blueprint for investing

*A*nother critical aspect of investing is the amount of money you put in each type of investment. While there is no magic answer, I will present in this chapter a blueprint for investing. The name given for how one distributes their investments is called asset allocation. Of course, it's not just important as to what you invest in, but an overall plan that has diversification will provide a lower risk investment plan. **Diversification is key to weathering the storms that may occur in the financial markets.**

I will now offer 4 categories of investments. Starting with category 1, these are the most secure and lowest risk investments. Category 2 investments offer a slightly higher risk and therefore generally have a little bit higher return. Likewise, category 3 investments are a slightly higher risk than category 2 investments and therefore generally could result in a higher return. Categories 4 investments are the highest risk investments that I am covering. It doesn't mean they're bad investments it just means that your portfolio should be weighted with each of the categories for investments appropriately. After reviewing the investments in each category I will go into more detail on what I believe, would be a proper allocation for the prudent investor.

Category 1

1. EE US government savings bonds.
2. CD's, FDIC insured.
3. Treasury securities.
4. Individual bonds above investment grade rating.
5. Close-end bond income funds with assets greater than 95% investment grade.
6. Open-end bond mutual funds with assets greater than 95% investment grade.
7. Preferred stock.

Category 2

1. Individual bonds with B grade rating or above.
2. Stocks that pay at least a 2.5% dividend for at least 10 years.
3. Closed-end income funds with assets greater than 50% investment-grade.
4. Open-end income mutual funds with assets greater than 50%

investment-grade.

5. REIT's that hold assets as real estate and have consistent dividends for at least 5 years.

6. BDC's that have consistent dividends for at least five years.

<u>Category 3</u>

1. Covered call options.
2. Stocks that pay at least a 2% dividend for the last five years.
3. Royalty trusts that have paid dividends for at least five years.
4. All other BDC's.
5. All other REIT's.
6. All MLP's

<u>Category 4</u>

1. All other individual bonds above C rating.
2. All other options.
3. Stocks with no dividends.
4. Any other investment.

It's important for you to analyze the categories and the investment types. It should be clear by now that risk plays a very important role in the potential return that you will obtain from your investments. I believe it's important for the long-term health of your financial future to have a solid base in your investments. That is why I believe it is appropriate for those investors with assets less than $50,000, to only invest in category 1 assets. This may seem quite conservative to most individuals. However, if one invests their hard earned dollars in category 2 or category 3 investments before achieving a solid base, it is very possible this type of investor will never achieve financial stability. That's why I believe in picking investments from category 1, before moving on to the other categories. One might say, "I am a young person and willing to take the risk." This may be the case, but the odds are against this type of investor ever achieving stability, over the long haul.

Another reason why it's so important to obtain category 1 investments first, is to generate diversification in your portfolio. It's difficult to have diversification with a small amount of assets. As one's assets grow, it will be easier to diversify into the other category investments.

The $50,000 cut off that I had suggested, is not a magical number, but rather a general range of assets that should be considered adequate to establish a solid base. This figure was determined by allowing 5% maximum per investment entity. This allows the investor 20 different investments at $2500 per investment. Also, as one increases their assets it will take time to achieve $50,000. So really, a small investor starts with a very small amount of resources, probably a few thousand dollars. So it makes sense that you want to invest the hard earned money that you have into safe investments. So basically, about every $2000-$3000 that you save, can be invested in a category 1 investment knowing that your money is safe. After achieving approximately 15-20 of these investments, then you will have a solid diversified portfolio. You can reduce the number of investments by putting more money in an income fund, which brings diversification by itself.

After achieving your solid investment base, then it is appropriate to invest in category 2, 3, and 4 investments. It would be beneficial to invest in category 2 investments before moving to category 3 or 4. Likewise, after investing in a category 2 investments, it is appropriate to then invest in category 3 investments, and then finally a category 4 investment. Keep in mind that the risk increases as the categories increase. To continue a diversified well-balanced investment plan one should consider obtaining investments in category 2, 3, and 4 while always maintaining 50% of your assets from category 1 investments. Some services like Morningstar, has a rating system for each investment that can help you analyze its risk and appropriately categorize.

So assets from $50,000-$100,000 may be selected from category 2, 3, and 4. After that point in your assets, any additional assets should be invested in category 1 investments. So for example, if one achieves $180,000 in assets, then 50% or $90,000 should be from category 1 investments and $90,000 from category 2, 3, and 4 investments. The weighting of the categories 2-4 investments are really a personal choice. You can take as much risk as you feel comfortable with. The key is that you have a solid base with 50% of your assets. It may be preferable to split your 50% categories 2-4 investments into thirds. So under this scenario one would have 50% category 1 and 16 2/3 percent categories 2-4. Like I said, the weighting in category 2-4 is a personal choice; however, it may not be prudent to weight all of your 50% investments in category 4. Although, with your category 1 investments, you have that choice.

There are many, many other investment choices that I have not gone into; which doesn't mean you shouldn't invest in them. Remember the fun of investing is researching. After you have achieved some level of assets and knowledge, you will be in a better position to make your own judgment on other investments.

In summary, I hope you have found my blueprint for investing to be educational. It is intended to be a guide for your financial future. But like any blueprint, you may find that a tweak here or there is more appropriate for your situation. **If you stick to lower risk, secure investments, in the beginning, you are bound to achieve a happier and healthier financial future.**

Blueprint synopsis.

Less than $50K assets   Category 1 investments only

Greater than $50K assets Category 1   50% of assets

                                         Categories 2-4 50% of assets

Chapter 7

Meet your broker on-line

As I said in an earlier chapter, computers and computer software advancements over the past 10 years have made it easier for the investor. The house, that will hold your investments, allow you to purchase and research your investments, and monitor their performance, will be your discount online brokerage account. There are many online brokerage companies that offer a full range of services that will allow you to adequately participate in all of the investments I have mentioned in this book, and then some. In addition, the pricing for purchasing CDs, stock, bonds, etc., are becoming exceedingly competitive. What use to cost hundreds of dollars to make a trade, now cost tens of dollars or less.

I have included a list of some of the more popular online brokerage account websites that are available. Forbes.com and other financial companies regularly evaluate online brokerage sites. This may be one source of information that will help you decide which brokerage website you would like to use. Before making your final decision, on which site to choose, go to their websites and run through their tutorials. You may also want to consider using multiple sites for your assets. I personally use at least three different brokerage sites for managing my assets. Sometimes one site may have some particular advantage over another. For example, one site may be stronger in bonds, such that, you would purchase the bulk of your bonds on that particular site. Another site, for example, may be stronger in displaying your portfolio. Some sites have the capabilities of adding phantom portfolios. Things like watch list, stock price barriers, third-party research tools, are just a few advantages one online broker may have over the other.

Today's online brokerage accounts are more than just buying and selling stocks and bonds. You can have access to your funds, through checking accounts. Your interest and dividend checks will be deposited directly to your money market or cash accounts. You will have instant visibility into your investment transactions. Most sites pay interest on your cash portion of your portfolio and allow you to choose from a wide range of taxable and tax-free money market choices.

Also when evaluating the web sites, don't be afraid to call and get help about the use of their sites. It doesn't cost you any money and they have a lot of free information to give. Most of the time they are willing to run through the process, on their sites, on how to make trades and purchase securities. Once you open an account think of them as your personal assistant.

In summary, do your research, pay attention to the fees being charged on your trades (usually the cost to purchase CD's are free), evaluate their capabilities, observe how they display your portfolio, and select a couple online discount brokers to manage your financial future.

\

Chapter 8

Advanced research

*I*n this chapter I will provide some additional detail when researching your investments. Hopefully, the online brokerage website that you have selected, will allow you to research your investments adequately. In a later chapter, I will also provide some third-party websites that may also be beneficial in helping you research your investments.

In the following examples, I have picked out a few key

points that are imperative when comparing and researching your potential investments.

Bond example:

Your online website should have capabilities for searching for live bonds. Live bonds search is merely a secondary market allowing buyers and sellers to come together for the purpose of bond exchange. After getting into the bond search screen, you should be able to search for the parameters that will help you to evaluate various bonds. For instance, you may want to put a minimum yield into the search field. You can then sort on yield, and this should return a number of bonds that are for sale. The list should give you the bond issuer, the coupon rate, the yield, and possibly the maturity date. To review the details of a particular bond, you should be able to click on the issuer. At that point, the bond offering detail should come up on your screen. I have included, typically, the information that will be displayed.

Bond Offering Detail

Issue: Home Depot Inc Sr Nt 5.875% 36 Make Whole Call Only - Listed

CUSIP/ISIN/SEDOL:
437076AS1/ US437076AS19/
B1L80H6

Type: Corporate

Coupon 5.875

Frequency: Semiannually

Maturity: 12/16/2036

First Coupon: 06/16/2007

First Settlement:

Next Coupon: 06/16/2007

Issue Date: 12/19/2006

Last Coupon: 06/16/2036

Collateral: Note

Minimum Amount: 1,000.00

Denomination Amount:
1,000.00

Blue Sky Requirements:

Moody/S&P: Aa3/A+

Category: Industrial

Delivery: Book Entry

Original Issue Size:
$3,000,000,000

Outstanding Issue Size:
$3,000,000,000

Issuer Full Name: The Home Depot, Inc. **Listed:** Y **Symbol:** HD

Offer

Price: 95.742	Settlement: 06/01/2007
Yield To Maturity: 6.19	Duration: 13.665
Yield To Call: -	Quantity: 500
Yield To Par: -	Increment: 1
Current Yield: 6.136	Min Quantity: 1
Worst Yield: Maturity	

  The first line shows the issue, this is the entity who is issuing the bonds. In this example, the corporate bond is issued by Home Depot. It's a Senior Note with a coupon rate of 5.875% and it will mature on December 16, 2036. The denomination of each bond is $1000 and the interest payments will be made semiannually, June 16 and December 16. We can see that Moody gives this a bond rating of Aa3, which is considered an investment grade bond. There are no calls to this bond so therefore, the holder will either sell this bond on the secondary market or hold it until its maturity. The price is at a discount, $95.742. This indicates a bond price of $957.42. Since it is at a discount, the yield that you will effectively obtain is 6.19%. If there was a call feature on this bond there would be a yield to call. The duration of 13.665 years indicates the amount of time necessary to recover your original investment. There are 500 bonds being offered and you must purchase them in increments of one. The minimum quantity that must be purchase is one. So in this example if one purchased one corporate bond it would cost $957.42, the accrued interest, from the last interest payment, and possibly a transaction fee.

This is the detail of the bond that is being offered. Of course, you would want to look at Home Depot's website, possibly see how their common stock is doing, under the ticker HD, and obtain any information you feel is necessary that would allow yourself to feel comfortable that Home Depot is going to be able to make its interest payments in the foreseeable future.

If you decide to purchase this bond, you will then click the buy button, enter your order, and then you'll be asked to review your order before placing the final order. It's important to review all information to make sure that it got entered as you thought it did. This is your last opportunity before the bond is purchased. Once you click purchase, it can take anywhere from instantly to minutes to even hours to fill your order. However, some websites may ask you make a phone call instead of buying directly online. This is one aspect of your website that you must review before utilizing its services.

You can review the status of the order, usually in the open orders page. Once the order has been executed it will be updated and all of the information about your bond including, accrued interest and transaction fees will be displayed.

Then just sit back and enjoy your investment and collect your interest's payments. Your interest payments will be automatically deposited into your account on June 16 and December 16, of every year until 2036.

REIT Example:

This example is for a real estate investment trust, called Healthcare. It is a REIT that invests in senior citizen facilities. I would like to point out a few details on the financial data for this REIT.

REITs are purchased on the open market similar to a common stock. After going to be their website and understanding the type of facilities, the location of their facilities, and reading about their company in general, you are ready to do research on your online brokerage website. There should be analyst research papers written on their financial performance. I have extracted some of that information from the Standard & Poor's financial analysis. In most cases, there should be more than one opinion offered by competing analyst. It's important to read through the various analyst valuations. The papers are usually four to five pages long, gives highlights details, potential stock price, explains their decisions, and usually offers an opinion.

Financial Data For Health Care REIT Ticker: HCN

Per Share Data ($)

Year Ended Dec. 31	2006	2005	2004	2003	2002
Tangible Book Value	27.04	19.85	24.23	20.43	19.20
Earnings	1.32	1.06	1.38	1.44	1.47
S&P Core Earnings	1.32	1.06	1.38	1.41	1.46
Dividends	**2.88**	**2.46**	**2.39**	**2.34**	**2.34**
Payout Ratio	NM	NM	173%	163%	159%
Prices:High	43.02	39.20	40.88	36.1	31.82
Prices:Low	32.80	31.15	27.70	24.8	24.02
P/E Ratio:High	33	37	30	25	22
P/E Ratio:Low	25	29	20	17	16

Per Share Data ($)

Year Ended Dec. 31	2001	2000	1999	1998	1997
Tangible Book Value	18.57	19.04	19.52	19.0	19.21
Earnings	1.52	1.91	2.21	2.24	2.12
S&P Core Earnings	1.51	NA	NA	NA	NA
Dividends	**2.34**	**2.34**	**2.27**	**2.19**	**2.11**
Payout Ratio	154%	122%	103%	98%	100%
Prices:High	26.40	19.25	26.63	29.2	28.75
Prices:Low	24.02	16.06	13.81	14.69	20.0
P/E Ratio:High	17	10	12	13	14
P/E Ratio:Low	11	7	7	9	10

The first thing that jumps out at you is that, they have been paying consistent and increasing dividends for over 10 years. This shows a huge commitment by the management of this company that they want to continue to be a good investment. For me, the dividend history and track record is very important. It at least shows me they are committed to increasing shareholder value. Of course, no one knows what's going to happen in the future, and it could change, the industry could change, no one knows for sure. So really, the only thing you have to go on is their track history.

Now looking further, there is some cause for concern because the payout ratio is quite high. You can see that the dividends are exceeding the earnings in some years. This could indicate that the finances are being stretched or they have been giving income from the sale of assets, or possibly from the offering of new stock. The high payout ratios, in itself, is not necessarily bad, however, it is important to understand where you're dividends are coming from. The analysis reports will give you insight into this aspect of the financials.

The share price history and P/E ratio is also given on this screen. This data along with the analysis will give you a good idea as to the potential for making their dividend payments.

Based on a review of the analysts reports I would

conclude this entity to be a category 2 investment. Of course, this is not a black or white decision. Someone may evaluate this entity and believe it should be a category 3 investment. This is where you add your value to the research. However, it's definitely not a category one investment. Remember, there are several REIT's to choose from so the process is comparing and choosing the best one that fits into your plan.

Royalty Trusts Example:

Pengrowth Energy Trust Ticker: PGH

Fiscal Year Ending	12/02	12/03	12//04	12//05	12/06
Sales (mil)	$378.6	$543.1	$619.9	$884.	$917.8
EPS (GAAP)	$0.75	$1.72	$1.24	$2.04	$0.90
Dividends/Share	**$1.92**	**$2.48**	**$2.43**	**$2.61**	**$2.78**
Book Value/Share	$8.99	$8.67	$8.85	$8.55	$11.57
Tangible Book Value/	$8.99	$8.67	$7.82	$7.49	$9.30
Cash Flow/Share	$2.53	$3.28	$2.98	$3.80	$3.49

Pengrowth is an energy oil trust. Royalty trusts are more difficult to evaluate and it is exceedingly important to read analyst reports before making your decision. Royalty trusts can provide a wonderful stream of income, but it is based most of the time, on the price of oil. If one believes that oil is a diminishing resource then it may be prudent to own a royalty trust.

Once again I have extracted some information from the Standard & Poor's analysis. The data shows that it has been paying increasing dividends over the last five years. Since the price of oil over the last five years has been increasing steadily, then it makes sense that the dividends should have been increasing. You will find after analyzing more royalty trusts, that nearly all have increasing dividends because of the price of oil. So in this case, this is not an advantage to Pengrowth, rather it should be considered a given for oil royalty trust at this time.

The book value per share has been consistent and this could be a cause for concern, however the cash flow has been increasing at a good pace.

You could not properly determine if Pengrowth is for you, just based on the financials given here.

The following additional information from Standard and Poor's analysis is given:

Key Operating Information:

Production for 2006 averaged 62,821 barrels of oil equivalent (boe) per day, a 6% increase from 2005, reflecting volumes added through the Carson Creek and Esprit Trust acquisitions and through ongoing development activities. At December 31, 2006, proved reserves were 225.9 million barrels of oil equivalent (mmboe) and proved plus probable reserves were 297.8 mmboe, an increase of 29% and 36%, respectively, from the reserves at the end of 2005. During 2006, on a proved plus probable basis, Pengrowth added 22.7 mmboe through drilling, improved recoveries and technical revisions and 81.5 mmboe through acquisitions. Additions were partially offset by 22.9 mmboe of production and 2.8 mmboe of divestitures.

In this example, being an oil trust, the proven reserves are very important. Over the past year, they have increased their reserves by 29%, through the acquisition of additional wells and development activities. It appears that they are continuing to increase their assets which are a very positive development. Since determining reserves is difficult scientifically, the reserves will change from year to year, up or down. You can see they also added reserves from technical revisions. It's important to monitor this parameter at least on a yearly basis or maybe even quarterly.

In summary only you can determine if Pengrowth or any other royalty trust is acceptable for your portfolio. However, with a little analysis, research on your part, you can obtain income from the energy sector.

I hope you have found these three examples educational and beneficial. Once again, researching, evaluating the opinions of others, and determining where investments properly fit in your financial plan is the essence of investing.

Chapter 9

Example Portfolio's

I will now show a $50,000 and $100,000 portfolio. The type of investments will be shown with approximate terms that can be expected at the time this book is being written. It's meant to serve as a guide for your investing sequence. It's difficult to start investing because one has little resources. This usually means that your first few investments are not diversified and therefore could be at risk. It's important to start investing in those instruments that will contribute to a safe and secure base portfolio. **So the sequence of the investments is**

also meant to aid in the safe accumulation of wealth.

The investment types will be annotated and it is up to you the investor, to research the various offerings available in each investment type. **Remember, not just any investment will do.** It's incumbent upon you, the investor, to adequately research and purchase the best investment that you can, evaluating risk and the potential return.

The $50,000 portfolio has individual bonds, as I indicated earlier; it's preferable to buy at a discount. So your real portfolio will have some cash, invested in a money market account, but for the purposes of this example, I have calculated the yearly income based on the face value, $1000, for each bond.

Another thing to remember, when purchasing individual bonds; you need to have bonds from various industries. In other words, I have shown 4 separate individual bonds that should be purchased from 4 different industries but each purchase will be 5 bonds.

$50,000 portfolio

<u>Category 1</u>

Investment type	Return	Value	Yearly Income
5 EE Savings Bonds	3.4%	$500FV	$8.50
Treasury security	4.8%	$2500	$120
CD-6 month	5.25%	$2000	$105
Closed-end fund	6.8%	$5000	$340
5-Individual Bonds-Aaa	6.0%	$5000	$300
Preferred Stock	6.8%	$5000	$340
5-Individual Bonds A	7%	$5000	$350
Closed-end fund	7%	$5000	$350
CD-1 Year	5.5%	$2000	$110
Dividend Paying stock	6.9%	$5000	$345
5-Individual Bonds A	7.1%	$5000	$355
5-Indivdual Bonds A	7.4%	$5000	$370
CD-1 Yr	5.6%	$3000	$112
Cash	2.5%	?	?

Totals	6.4%	$50000	$3205.50

The return percentages that I have shown are only hypothetical but are real returns as of the writing of this book. Your returns will vary based on the time that you make your investments. In most cases, these investments will be made over a period of years because it takes time to grow your wealth.

If someone already has achieved the $50000, and executes this type of portfolio, then the returns will still be subject to the interest rate environment at the time. Also, no need to rush in making investments, it's more important to analysis and learn as you go. Deposit the money into the cash account and do your research before making an investment.

In addition to the income produced by this portfolio, there is the real possibility that capital gain increases will occur because:

1. The bonds are bought at a discount.
2. The closed-end fund and preferred stock are market driven and could go up or down, however if held over time, they should eventually end up.

After achieving this $50,000, after 5 years it will be worth, approximately, $68,200, after 10 years it will be worth approximately, $93,000, and after 15 years it will be worth, approximately, $126,840, excluding taxes. These figures do not account for adding any money to the portfolio, so most likely you will achieve higher numbers if you continue your savings. Also taxes play a role in this accumulation of your wealth. If you are a young person and you fund your portfolio will odd jobs money, then you will not have to worry about taxes, since you will be below the income tax line. However as your salary increases, taxes will become a consideration that needs to be addressed. Since you may have additional income combined with your investment income, your normal withholding may not be sufficient. **It is always better to get as much money as possible saved early in your life, and pay taxes on the income, because it will compound much quicker.** Here are some choices you have, to deal with the taxes on your investment income.

1. Offset the income with additional deductions (Maybe volunteer and donate).
2. Pay the taxes out of the investment income (This will reduce your wealth accumulation).
3. Switch some of your investments to tax free bonds.
4. Reduce your savings rate and pay the taxes from your salary.

Remember, the faster you get your money into your portfolio, the faster it will accumulate, even if you have to decrease your savings rate in later years. This is contrary to what most people do. They start to increase their contributions later in life. While it's never too late, if you're young, you have the chance to have it easier, later in life.

100,000 Portfolio

Category 1

$50,000 as invested from above

Category 2

Preferred Stock	$5,000
REIT	$5,000
BDC	$5,000
REIT	$5,000

Category 3

Royalty Trust	$5,000
Dividend Paying stock	$5,000
Royalty Trust	$5,000
Dividend Paying stock	$5,000

Category 4

Stock with no Dividend	$5,000
5-Individual bonds - B grade	$5,000
Subtotals	$50,000
Totals	$100,000

The returns will vary greatly as you invest in category 2-4 investments, so it's not beneficial to predict the outcomes or potential returns. Refer back to the categories when determining the type of investment you are looking to make. A category 3 REIT is a higher risk, than a category 2 REIT, because of the tack record or any other worries you may find. **But remember, not any investment will do.** The category 4 bonds may not be that solid, you may not hold them for a long time, but you should get a very high return. A calculated risk in this area may be a company that has a great product, but are in temporary financial difficulties.

Taxes play a bigger role as you increase your wealth and investment income. Switching some investments into tax free bonds or funds may be appropriate. Also I did not show an MLP in the portfolio, but one can achieve tax advantages when investing in them. So you could substitute an MLP in place of one of the REITS. MLP's are legal tax shelters, registered as such, but require additional tax paperwork (K-1's) when doing your tax returns, which make it a little more complicated.

Chapter 10

You And Your Websites

*T*he computer, and software, over the last 10 years, has made investing, and the management of your investments, considerably easier. This chapter will offer the websites that can be used, actually, are imperative, to the investor. I'm hesitant, of course, to include this type of information in printed form. As one knows, websites change. So probably in 5 or 10 years if you're reading this book, this chapter may have less importance. I will try to give details of the websites so that if the actual website address has changed you will be able to type in keywords to find the same type of information.

Online brokerages:

http://bankofamerica.com/investing   Bank of America

http://www.scottrade.com   Scottrade

http://www.tdameritrade.com   TD Ameritrade

http://www.etrade.com   Etrade

http://www.schwab.com   Charles Schwab

This is only a partial list of full service online brokerages. It's important to find one that you are comfortable with, and always review their fee structure.

Closed-end funds:

www.closed-endfunds.com

This link takes you to the Closed-End Fund Association. They have free literature, links to other sites, and more importantly, a screener that allows you to review all 693(number at this writing) Closed End Funds.

Open-end funds (mutual funds):

http://www.morningstar.com

Your online brokerage should have enough information for you to make a choice in mutual funds. However you may also want to use Morningstar, they seem to have a tremendous amount of information on mutual funds. They also have a rating system for stocks.

EE savings bonds:

http://www.treasurydirect.gov

This is the US government's own website for buying all kinds of securities, including EE bonds. You need to open an account before you can purchase. Most banks also offer the capabilities to purchase EE savings bonds.

http://www.treasurydirect.gov/BC/SBCPrice

This link provides direct access to the bond calculator. You can get the exact value of your bonds on this page by inputting the bond serial number and issue date. Both are on the face of the bond.

Real estate investment trust (REIT's):

There are 198 REIT's that are currently listed on the exchanges. The best source for researching RIET's is quantum online. Your brokerage should also provide you access to research information from analyst reports.

Royalty trusts:

There are 24 US and 45 Canadian Royalty trusts listed for review. The best source is http://www.quantumonline.com or your brokerage site.

Business development corporations (BDC's):

There are currently 25 BDC's listed for review. The best site is
http://www.quantumonline.com or your brokerage website.

Mater Limited Partnerships (MLP's):

There are currently 69 MLP's listed for review. The best site is
www://quantum online.com or your brokerage website.

Third-party online tools:

http://www.quantumonline.com

This is the best website I that I have found for researching
income type investments. You can sign up for free, it only asks
for donations. It is very comprehensive in many income type
investments, including others that I did not mention.

http://www.moodys.com

The basic service is free, which provides nearly all of the
information you will need to research your bonds. Here you
will be able to monitor the bond ratings and obtain the rational
for the ratings. You can access the information by either the
CUSIP or the issuer's name. The ratings don't change that
often, checking every 1-2 months should be sufficient. Your
brokerage may also offer alerts when the ratings change, which
is easier.

http://www.bloomberg.com/markets/rates

Bloomberg has a lot of general market information at their
homepage. The link I have provided goes directly to the Yield

Curve. This is an important parameter to monitor, because this will give you an idea where interest rates stand. You can expect CD and Aaa bonds will be slightly higher than the US treasury yields.

Newsletters:

I have subscribed over the years to many newsletters; I offer 2 that may be beneficial to the income type investor. I get them delivered to my home but also have access on their website. They are not required but may give some good ideas when tying to research investments. Usually they cost less than $100 per year.

High Yield Investing, http://www.streetauthority.com
They have multiple newsletters, but the one I like is called High Yield Investing. It has a lot of ideas on income type investments that pay a dividend.

Personal Finance, http://www.pfnewsletter.com
This is a general newsletter, but the editor has good insight into income investments.

Chandler Deyo Email:

Lastly I want to provide an email address where I can be reached to answer any questions. I don't know everything about investing, so sometimes a simple, "I don't know may result". Also if you find mistakes or would like to offer criticism, I will be listening.

Qwbs67@msn.com

Chapter 11

401 Type Accounts

*M*any corporations today offer their employees the opportunity to invest in tax deferred accounts, known as 401's, or something similar. Most employees get money taken out of their paychecks, before taxes, and are allowed to put it in a managed account, with the recipient allowed to make some choices on the type of investments. Most companies utilize an experienced money management firm to run their 401. The types of investments vary greatly from plan to plan. So the employee is stuck with whatever investments are offered.

However, from my experience, at least, a broad range of instruments are offered. You may be limited on the number of investments, but you should still be able to invest in the type of investments that I mentioned here. So for instance, you might have a closed-end fund or bond fund to invest in. You would want to have similar kinds of mixes that I have mentioned, 50% secure, in bond or income type investments and then more aggressive type investments. Some 401's even offer REITS. Since 401's are tax deferred, I would agree that a heavier weight after the first 50% of assets could come from mutual funds.

Usually after leaving a company, you are allowed to move your assets into a self directed brokerage account. At that point you will be allowed to make investments in anything you desire.

Don't forget however, these are not tax free investments. They only grow tax free until you have to take them out, then you must pay taxes. You should keep this in the back of your mind as your salary and investments start to grow.

Chapter 12

Tickers, Tickers, Tickers

I am providing the tickers for some of the categories of investments that I have reviewed. This is not a recommended list to buy, just a list, by category of the companies available. Tickers can change, so in time some of them will not be valid. Also when a company goes into bankruptcy, they sometimes change the ticker or add a letter.

US Royalty Trusts

Total list of 24. There are an additional 45 Canadian trusts.

BPT	COCBF	CRT	DOM	NGT
GNI	HGT	LRT	MARPS	MDSH
MTR	MSB	MMTRS	NRT	PHX
PBT	SBR	SJT	SFF	TELOZ
TISDZ	TRU	TISDZ	WTU	

Business Development Corps (BDC's)
Total list of 25.

ALD	AFC	ACAS	AMTC	AINV
ARCC	BBDC	CSWC	EQS	FKL
GLAD	GAIN	TINY	HTGC	MACC
MCGC	TAXI	MVC	NGPC	PSEC
RAND	RCG	UTK	WSCC	WCAP

Master Limited Partnerships (MLP's)
Total list of 69.

ARLP	AB	ATAXZ	ACP	APU
XXAAU	AHD	APL	BWP	BCPUQ
BGH	BPL	FUN	CQP	CEP
CPNO	XTEX	DPM	DMLP	EEQ
EEP	ETE	ETP	EPD	EPCPF
EQUUS	FGP	XXFPC	FCGYF	GEL
GLP	HTLLQ	HLND	HEP	NRGP
NRGY	IPPLF	KMP	KMR	KSP
LAACZ	LAZ	MGC	MMP	MWE
MMLP	NUT	MMA	NRP	NSP
NEW	OKS	PPX	PVR	PAA
POPEZ	RVEP	SGU	STON	SPH
SXL	TCLP	TGP	TPP	TNH
TLP	USS	WPC	WPZ	

Real-estate Investment Trusts (REIT's)
Partial list of the 193 total.

AKR	ARC	ALX	AMB	APRO
ACC	AHM	AMC	NLY	AHR
AUB	BMR	BXP	CMO	CDR
DRE	EQR	GLB	GTA	HCP
HCN	HR	HTG	HPT	HST
IMH	SFI	MPW	MFA	NHI
OHI	PEI	PCL	PSA	SNH
UHT	VNO	WXH		

Chapter 13

The end of the beginning.

*W*ell this is the end of our journey for this book. I hope you enjoyed it and found it educational. I think I met my objectives, at least I hope I did.

If you are my wife, daughter, son, mother, father, sister, nephew, niece, in-law or friend, and you are reading this book,

I hope you have all the opportunities that I've had, to meet your financial goals.

Remember, money in itself doesn't bring happiness. Your independent wealth, at whatever level, provides security and some self-sufficiency and independence. I wish you good fortune in your research of your investments, **because not just any investment will do**.

Now go out and create your own financial story.

Happy investing!

Chandler Deyo

Think about your goals and write them down.

Notes

O'Reilly, Bill. Who's Looking Out for You?. New York: Broadway Books, 2003.

Anderson, Brett & Thomas Kostigen. "100 Year Plan Part I: The Family Mission Statement." Worth 1 Dec. 2003.

Rates & Bonds. Bloomberg. 18 July 2007
http://www.bloomberg.com/markets/rates/index.html.

The Dividend Rediscovered. Thornburg Investment Management. 4 June 2007
http://www.thornburginvestments.com/research/articles/Rediscovered_Dividends.asp

Confidence Intervals for Corporate Default Rates. April 2007. Moody's Investors Service.
http://www.moodys.com/moodys/cust/research/MDCdocs/04/2006600000426807.pdf?doc_id=2006600000426807&frameOfRef=corporate

Moody's Rating System. May 2006. Moody's Investors Service.
http://www.moodys.com/moodys/cust/research/mdcdocs/24/2005700000433096.pdf

Dividend History. General Electric. 18 July 2007
http://www.ge.com/investors/stock_info/dividend_history.html

United States. United States Courts. Bankruptcy Basics, April 2004.

Highlighted quotes from the book.

1. Pg. 2. For me and other investors, this is the fun of investing. Researching your investment, assessing the risk, and getting a periodic return.

2. Pg. 9. We can obtain advice, we can learn from others' mistakes, but we must take responsibility for our financial future.

3. Pg. 10. It's important to understand that we live in a capitalistic society where we are allowed to participate in the fruits of our workers and producers.

4. Pg. 15. If on the other hand, if the stock has increased because of an increased dividend, then the increase is, so-called bought and paid for.

5. Pg. 16. In summary, to achieve the long-term goal of having personal responsibility through financial success in investing, it is essential that investments be made in those entities that provide a return through dividend or interest payments.

6. Pg. 18. I want you to understand that you have a financial life, not an addition to your normal life but one that should be in concert with your normal life.

7. Pg. 24. In my mind it was crystal clear; the way to total self dependency was through savings.

8. Pg. 26. The more you can save in the early years, the earlier it will be in later years that you will meet your goals.

9. Pg. 28. That's really the way you have to look at it. How much security are you able to bring to yourself.

10. Pg. 31. The bottom line here is this; it's not important why interest rates go up and down, what you need to know as an investor is, how the change affects your investments.

11. Pg. 32. Bonds or bond funds are going to decrease in value when interest rates rise and increase in value when interest rates fall.

12. Pg. 33. In other words, if you buy individual bonds and intend to hold them until maturity, then you don't have to worry about interest rates.

13. Pg. 34. Just because the bonds are rated junk doesn't mean the companies that issue those bonds are junk.

14. Pg. 38. So if bonds are purchased at discount, the rate of return will be higher than the coupon rate.

15. Pg. 41. Closed-end income funds are a good investment for someone who needs to preserve capital and obtain high income.

16. Pg. 45. However keep in mind that a low return in all cases is better than a negative return and possibly the loss of capital.

17. Pg. 48. If interest rates go down during the period of the bond, it would be better to buy EE bonds, if interest rates go up during that period, it would be better to buy I bonds.

18. Pg. 52. The inherent basic principle of preferred stock gives a very stable unit price with a high level of security providing income.

19. Pg. 53. It can therefore be asserted that it is much more secure and manageable if one follows an investment stock that pays dividends.

20. Pg. 56. The price of a stock is directly tied to the dividend and will move as the dividend moves.

21. Pg. 59. Sticking with REIT's that own property is a safer way to go, rather than those REIT's that hold loans on properties, until you have understood the nuances of this type of investment.

22. Pg. 59. Overall, real-estate provides many advantages to an investor and REITs are great means for the small investor to get a piece of this industry.

23. Pg. 60. So income that is distributed to the limited partners are mostly offset by deductions, which means the income realistically is tax-deferred until you sell the units or could even be tax-free.

24. Pg. 61. Like any other energy asset, as oil becomes more and more depleted, MLPs will be more valuable.

25. Pg. 62. Royalty trusts generally have a very high rate of return, four to six points above the treasury rates, at least.

26. Pg. 63. A key point in analyzing oil royalty reserves is the depletion timetables.

27. Pg. 68. In summary, covered call options can provide instant cash and can be a rewarding and profitable investing vehicle.

28. Pg. 69. Covered calls are a 100% guaranteed investment.

29. Pg. 79. Diversification is key to weathering the storms that may occur in the financial markets.

30. Pg. 83. If you stick to lower risk, secure investments, in the beginning, you are bound to achieve a happier and healthier financial future.

31. Pg. 98. So the sequence of the investments is also meant to aid in the safe accumulation of wealth.

32. Pg. 98. Remember, not just any investment will do.

33. Pg. 101. It is always better to get as much money as possible saved early in your life, and pay taxes on income, because it will compound much quicker.

34. Pg. 101. Remember, the faster you get your money into your portfolio, the faster it will accumulate, even if you have to decrease your savings rate in later years.

35. Pg. 103. But remember, not any investment will do.

36. Pg. 116. Because not just any investment will do.

www.ingramcontent.com/pod-product-compliance
Lightning Source LLC
Chambersburg PA
CBHW032008190326
41520CB00007B/394